RESTRICTED

RECOGNITION
OF
AIRBORNE EQUIPMENT

M.I. 10.
WAR OFFICE.
JUNE 1951.

The Naval & Military Press Ltd

Published by
The Naval & Military Press Ltd
5 Riverside, Brambleside, Bellbrook
Industrial Estate, Uckfield, East Sussex,
TN22 1QQ England
Tel: +44 (0) 1825 749494
Fax: +44 (0) 1825 765701
www.naval-military-press.com
www.military-genealogy.com
www.militarymaproom.com

In reprinting in facsimile from the original, any imperfections are inevitably reproduced and the quality may fall short of modern type and cartographic standards.

AIRBORNE RECOGNITION MANUAL

INSTRUCTIONS

1. As many different types of Airborne equipment and techniques both past and present are shown to enable readers:

    (a) To gain a background knowledge. Each section endeavours to show the whole history of development of that particular aspect.

    (b) To interrogate and debrief sources of information either by:

    (i) Simple recognition.
    (ii) Recognition by elimination.
    (iii) An intelligent use of the photographs to illustrate a technique or an equipment which is not shown.

    It should be appreciated that this manual by no means exhausts all the possibilities of aerial delivery; remembering that only practical and efficient methods are standardised and only standardisation makes large scale airborne assault possible.

2. In order to keep the classification as low as possible each page has been treated separately. If recipients wish to down grade the manual as a whole, the higher classification pages may be removed and held separately.

3. The picture captions are printed at the foot of each page so that they may be easily cut off by a recipient who so wishes. Untitled illustrations are often necessary for interrogation purposes in order to assess a source's degree of knowledge and reliability. An Index is provided for reference and the page numbers are arranged to coincide with the Figure numbers for the sake of convenience.

4. Each section has a coloured fly sheet and has a separate set of page numbers with its own picture caption index.

GENERAL INDEX TO SECTIONS

Section I	(Pink)	Transport Aircraft
Section II	(Yellow)	Military Gliders
Section III	(Green)	Parachutes
Section IV	(Brown)	Parachute Harness and Clothing
Section V	(Blue)	Airborne Containers
Section VI	(Grey)	Heavy dropping techniques
Section VII	(Red)	Airfreighting Accessories

SECTION I

AIRCRAFT

SECTION I TRANSPORT AIRCRAFT

This section is only representative of some of the military transport aircraft in use in the world to-day. The section is divided into two sub-sections. These and their order of arrangement are:

    (a)   Fixed Wing Aircraft

        (i)   Side loading aircraft - cargo and paratrooping.
        (ii)   Nose loading " - cargo only.
        (iii) Tail loading " - cargo, heavy dropping and paratrooping.
        (iv)   Pod carrying " - cargo only.

    (b)   Rotary Wing Aircraft - Helicopters.

        Only a few examples of these are shown as development of this type of aircraft for military uses is still very experimental. The many types and designs are very diverse although all are intended for freighting troops and cargo only.

A further type of aircraft "The Convertiplane" is in the design stage only; it will have the features of both fixed wing (horizontal speed) and rotary wing (vertical lift) aircraft.

SECTION I   TRANSPORT AIRCRAFT

Index:

(a)   Fixed Aircraft

   (i) Fig 1   German   JU-52/3m (Land)
        Fig 2   Russian   LI-2 (PS-84) - Copy of DAKOTA
        Fig 3   Russian   IL-12 military version
        Fig 4   British   HASTINGS C Mk-1 (Handley-Page)
        Fig 5   Russian   TU-70

  (ii) Fig 6   British   FREIGHTER 21 (Bristol)
        Fig 7   U.S.A.   GLOBEMASTER 2 (C-124)

 (iii) Fig 8   French   NORATLAS-NORD 2500
        Fig 9   French   BREGUET 76 - 1
        Fig 10 British   BLACKBURN Freighter (GAL)
        Fig 11 U.S.A.   PACKET C-119 (Fairchild)

  (iv) Fig 12 U.S.A.   PACK PLANE XC-120 (Fairchild)

(b)   Rotary Wing Aircraft

        Fig 13 Russian   BRATUSHKIN Helicopter
        Fig 14 British   CIERVA AIR HORSE W.II.
        Fig 15 U.S.A.   XH-17 (Flying $2\frac{1}{2}$ ton truck)

I/1

I TRANSPORT AIRCRAFT

(a) Fixed Wing Aircraft (i)

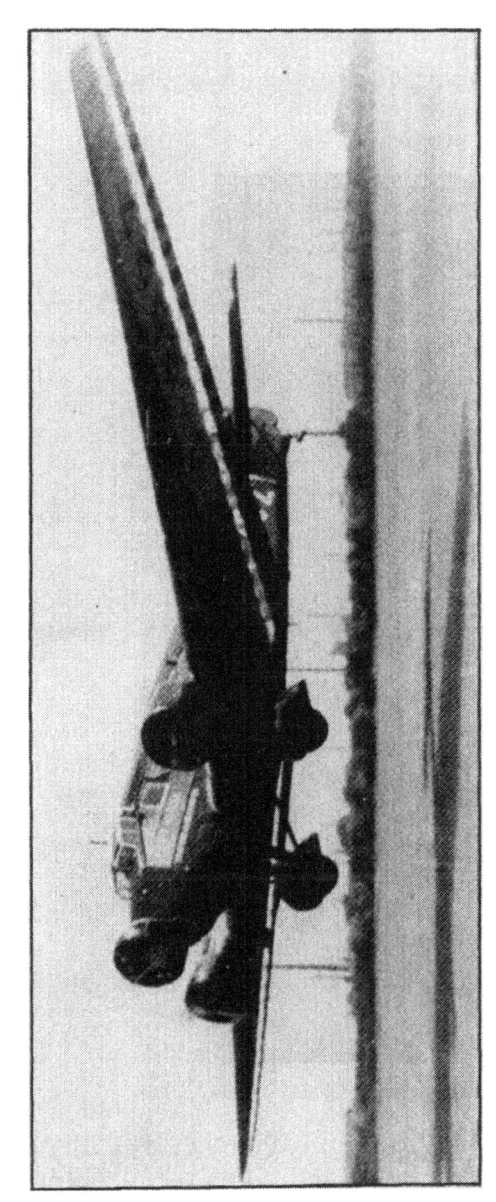

Wing Span :- 96 ft.   Length :- 62 ft.

Military Payload :- 4,070 lbs.

Special Features :- Loading by side door

Fig. 1   German   JU-52/3m   (Land)

RESTRICTED

I   TRANSPORT AIRCRAFT

(a) Fixed Wing Aircraft (i)

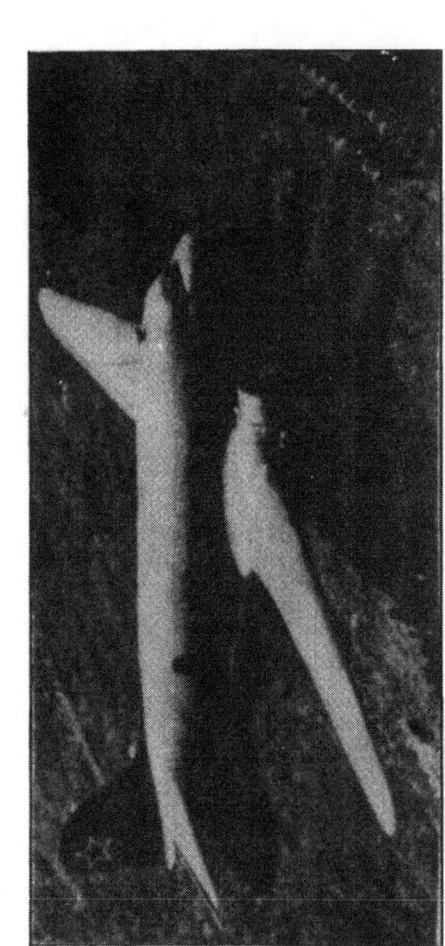

Wing Span :- 94¾ ft.   Length :- 63 ft.

Military Payload :- 6,600 lbs.

Special Features :- Some models fitted with starboard as well as port door for double door jumping. Some models also fitted with fuselage turret.

Fig. 2   Russian L1-2 (PS-84) - Copy of "Dakota"

RESTRICTED

I TRANSPORT AIRCRAFT

(a) Fixed Wing Aircraft (i)

Wing Span :- 104 ft.   Length :- 70 ft.
Military Payload :- 8,800 lbs.

Special Features :- Port side Cargo door $7\frac{1}{2}$ ft. wide. Probably carries heavy equipments, under fuselage, which may be dropped by parachute.

Fig. 3.   Russian IL-12   (Military Version)

I/3

I TRANSPORT AIRCRAFT

(a) Fixed Wing Aircraft (i)

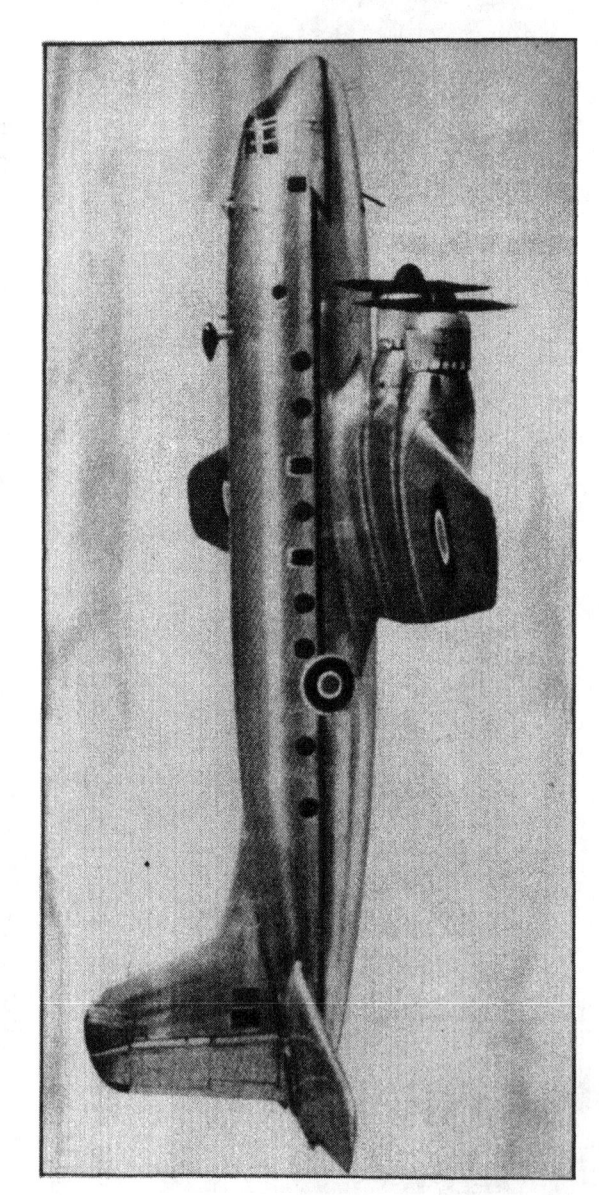

Wing Span :- 113 ft.   Length :- 82 ft.

Military Payload :- 16,000 lbs.

Special Features :- Side loading only. Port and starboard doors for double door jumping.

Fig. 4, British Handley Page **HASTINGS** C. Mk-1

RESTRICTED

I TRANSPORT AIRCRAFT

(a) Fixed Wing Aircraft (i)

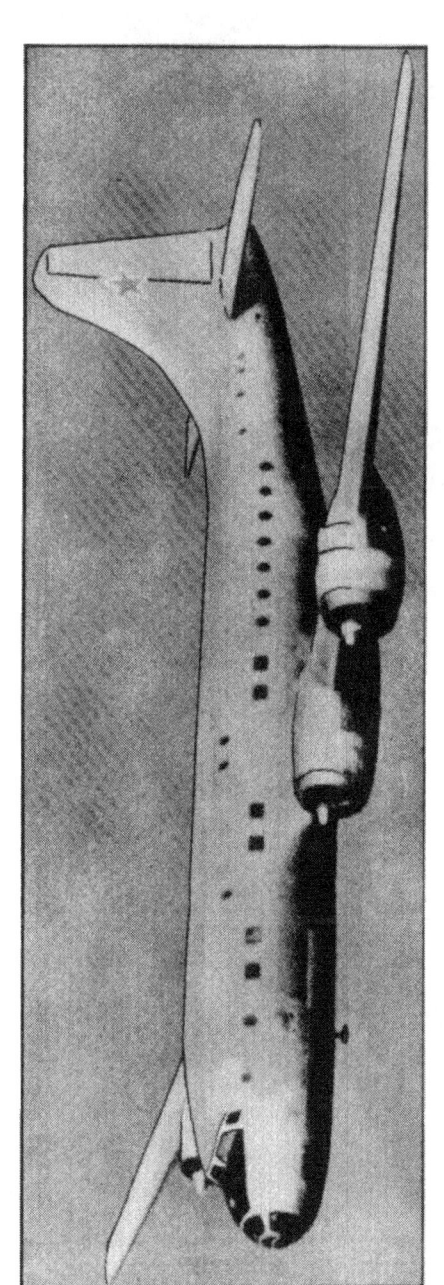

Wing Span :- 141.25 ft. Length :- 99 ft.

Military Payload :- 20,000 lbs.

Special Features :- Transport version of Russian TU-4 bomber which is a copy of B29 American Superfortress.

Fig. 5   Russian TU-70

I/5

I TRANSPORT AIRCRAFT

(a) Fixed Wing Aircraft (ii)

Wing Span :- 108'   Length :- $68\frac{1}{3}$ ft.
Military Payload :-   13,000 lbs.
Special Features :-   Loading doors in nose

Fig. 6   Bristol FREIGHTER 21

I/7

I   TRANSPORT AIRCRAFT

(a) Fixed Wing Aircraft (ii)

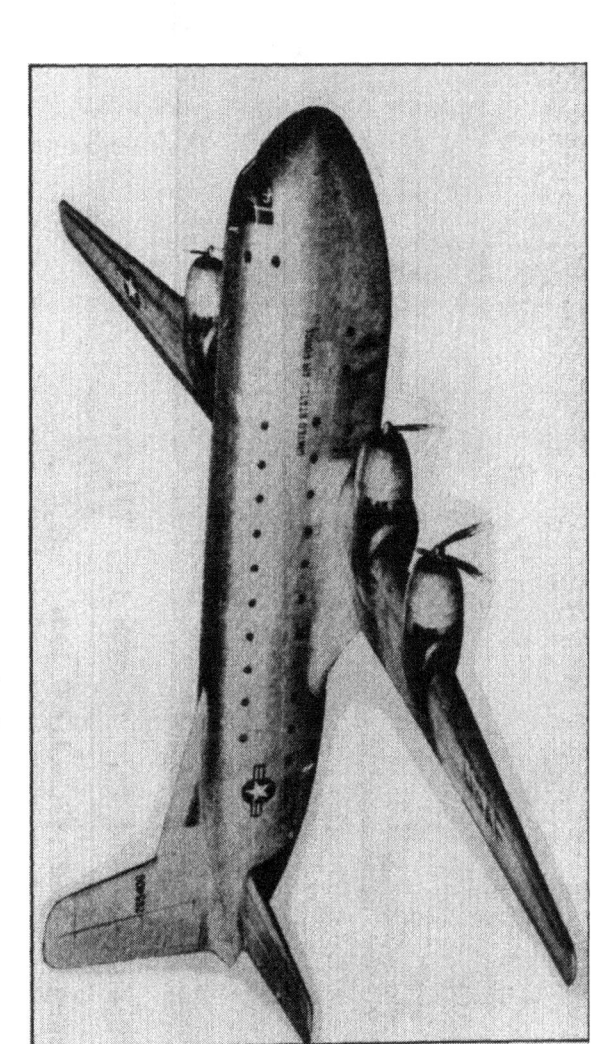

Wing Span :- 173¼   Length :- 127 ft.

Military Payload :- 50,000 lbs.

Special Features :- Nose doors lower to form ramps. Loading also possible through hatches. Equipped with power winches and lifts.

Fig. 7   U.S.A. Globemaster 2   C-124

RESTRICTED

I TRANSPORT AIRCRAFT

(a) Fixed Wing Aircraft (iii)

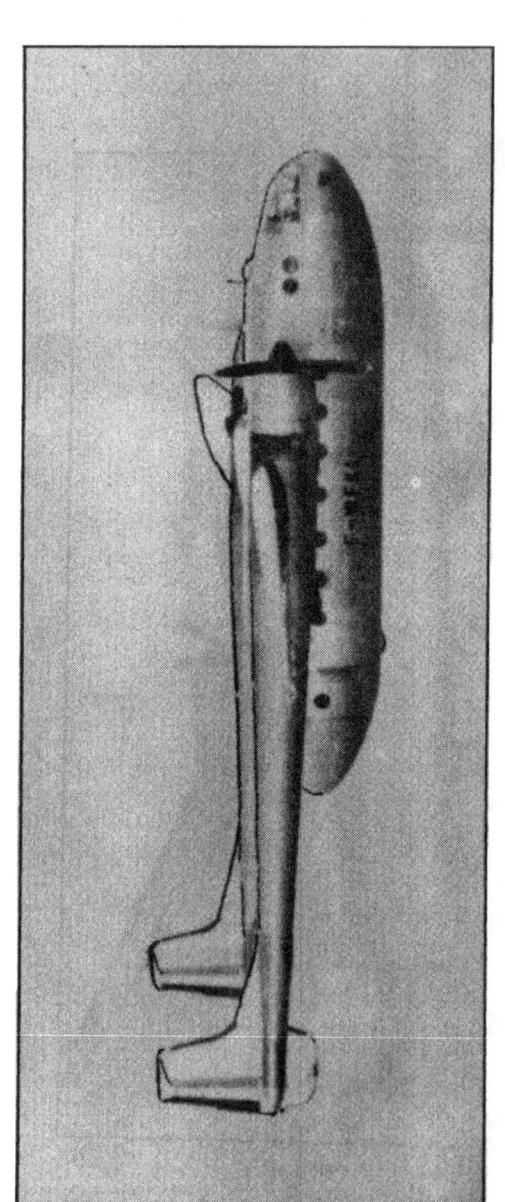

Wing Span :- $106\frac{1}{2}$ ft. Length :- $71\frac{1}{2}$ ft.

Military Payload :- 7,700 lbs.

Special Features :- Tail loading. Hatches also for parachuting containers.

Fig. 8   French Nord   2500 NORATLAS

RESTRICTED

I   TRANSPORT AIRCRAFT

(a) Fixed Wing Aircraft (iii)

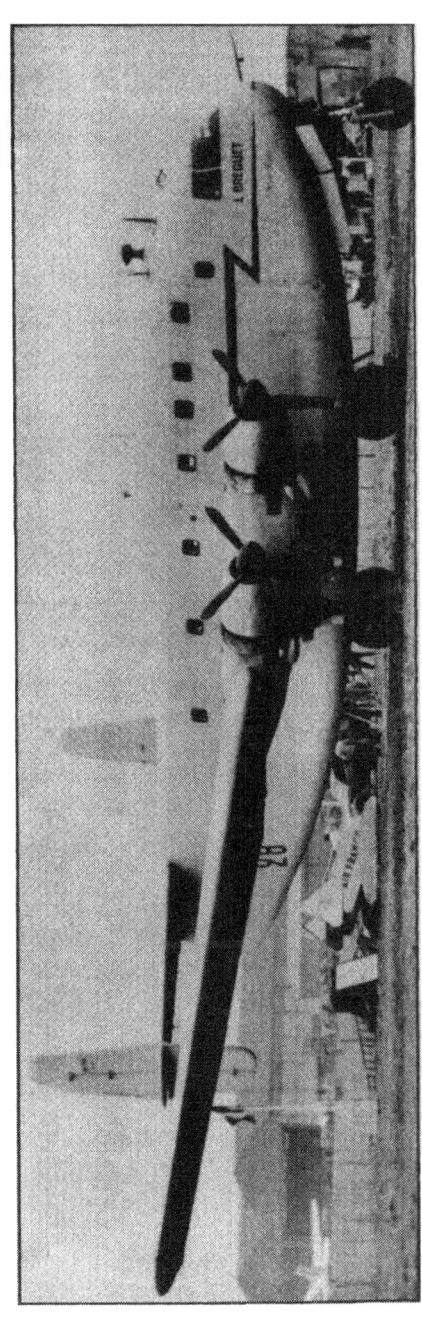

Wing Span :- 141 ft.   Length :- 95 ft.

Military Payload :- 29,000 lbs.

Special Features :- Loading by large doors in underside of fuselage near tail. Fuselage has two decks and can accommodate 100 paratroops.

Fig. 9   French   BREGUET 76-1

I/9

I TRANSPORT AIRCRAFT

(a) Fixed Wing Aircraft (iii)

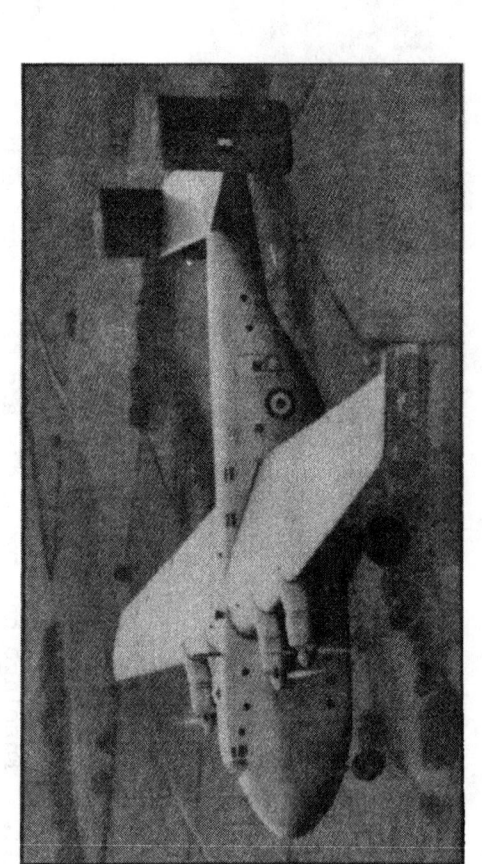

Wing Span :- 162 ft.   Length :- 99 ft.

Military Payload :- 33,000 lbs.

Special Features :- Tail loading doors incorporating ramps. There is a removable second deck.

Fig. 10   British BLACKBURN GAL Freighter

I   TRANSPORT AIRCRAFT

(a) Fixed Wing Aircraft (iii)

Wing Span :- $109\frac{1}{4}$ ft.   Length :-   86 ft.

Military Payload :-   30,000 lbs.

Special Features :- Tail loading and parachuting doors, Forward hatch for parachuting containers.

Fig. 11   U.S.A.   Packet C-119 (Fairchild)

I   TRANSPORT AIRCRAFT   I/12

(a) Fixed Wing Aircraft (iv)

9 tons (approx.)   Military pay-load

Special Features :-   A detachable fuselage or "Pod".
On depositing one pod the plane may return for another.

Fig. 12   U.S.A. Fairchild "Pack Plane" XC-120

RESTRICTED   I/13

I   TRANSPORT AIRCRAFT

(b)   Rotary Wing Aircraft

Military Payload :-   Carries 8 persons

Special Features :-

Fig. 13   Russian BRATUSHKIN Helicopter

I/14

I   TRANSPORT AIRCRAFT

(b) Rotary Wing Aircraft

Length :- 83 ft. (overall incl. rotors)

Military Payload :- over 2 tons

Special Features :- End loading doors

Fig. 14 British Cierva "AIR-HORSE" W.II

I/15

I TRANSPORT AIRCRAFT

(b) Rotary Wing Aircraft

Length :- $53\frac{1}{4}$ ft.   Diameter of rotating wing 130 ft.
Military Payload :- 10,284 lbs.
Special Features :- The underslung box, 9' x 9' x 20', is detachable.
    Fig. 15   U.S.A.   XH-17   (Flying $2\frac{1}{2}$ ton Truck)

SECTION II

GLIDERS

SECTION II   MILITARY GLIDERS

This section is more complete and gives most of the popular types used by all countries during World War II and since.

   (a)   Gliders (unpowered)

          (i)   Side loading Transport Gliders
          (ii) Nose loading Transport Gliders

          (iii) Tail loading Transport Gliders.

   These in turn have been graded according to size.

(b) Powered Gliders

   Basically a glider - a lightly constructed aircraft with a high wing span/length ratio, - incorporating power units to give it a greater performance in the air. Many of the types are merely standard gliders with engines. The assault aircraft is not a glider type really. Although it has the versatile landing characteristics of a glider, it does not require assistance for take-off.

SECTION II   MILITARY GLIDERS

Index:-

(a)   Gliders (unpowered)

  (i)   Fig 1   Russian   A.7.
         Fig 2   Japanese   KU.8.
         Fig 3   German   DFS.230
         Fig 4   Russian   KZ-20
         Fig 5   Swedish   FL-3

  (ii)   Fig 6   Russian   Type 25
         Fig 7   Russian   Type 24
         Fig 8   British   HORSA
         Fig 9   French   CM.10
         Fig 10   British   HAMILCAR
         Fig 11   German   ME 321 (Gigant)

  (iii) Fig 12   German   GOTHA 242
         Fig 13   U.S.A.   XCG-18A (chase)

(b)   Powered Gliders

         Fig 14   German   GOTHA 244
         Fig 15   German   ME 323
         Fig 16   British   HAMILCAR X
         Fig 17   U.S.A.   Chase XCG-123 (Assault aircraft)

II/1

II   MILITARY GLIDERS

(a)   Gliders (unpowered) (i)

Wing Span :-   59 ft.   Length :- $34\tfrac{1}{2}$ ft.

Military Payload :- 1,870 lbs.   Towing Aircraft :- L1-2

Special Features :- Loading by side door.   Retractable main undercarriage.   Skids for rough landing.

Fig. 1   Russian A.7 Glider

II MILITARY GLIDERS

(a) Gliders (unpowered) (i)

Wing Span :- 71 ft.   Length :- 43¾ ft.

Military Payload :- 3,600 lb. (approx.)

Special Features :- **Nose** loading

Fig. 2   Japanese KU-8 Glider

II MILITARY GLIDERS

(a) Gliders (unpowered) (i)

Wing Span :- $72\frac{1}{3}$ ft. Length :- $37\frac{1}{2}$ ft.
Military Payload :- 2,800 lbs. Towing Aircraft :- JU-52
Special Features :- Side loading

Fig. 3   German   DFS - 230   Glider

RESTRICTED

II MILITARY GLIDERS

(a) Gliders (unpowered) (i)

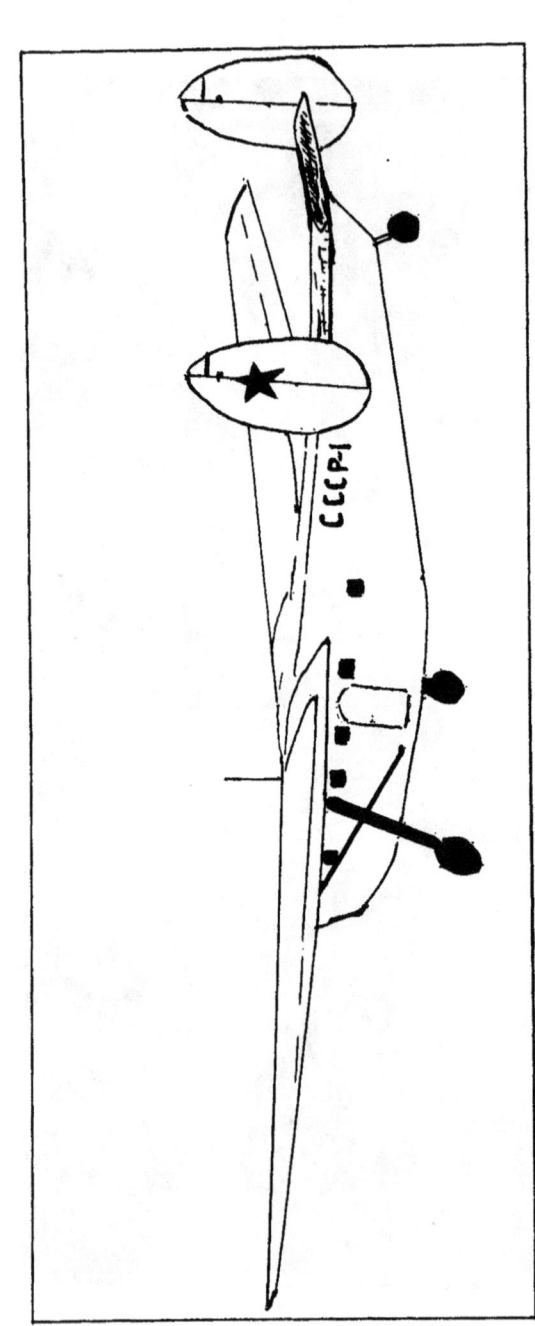

Wing Span :- 72 ft.   Length :- 50 ft.

Military Payload :- 3,600 lbs.

Special Features :- This glider fitted with two power units is called SHCHE-2. Side loading door.

Fig. 4 Russian KZ-20 Glider

II MILITARY GLIDERS

(a) Gliders (unpowered) (i)

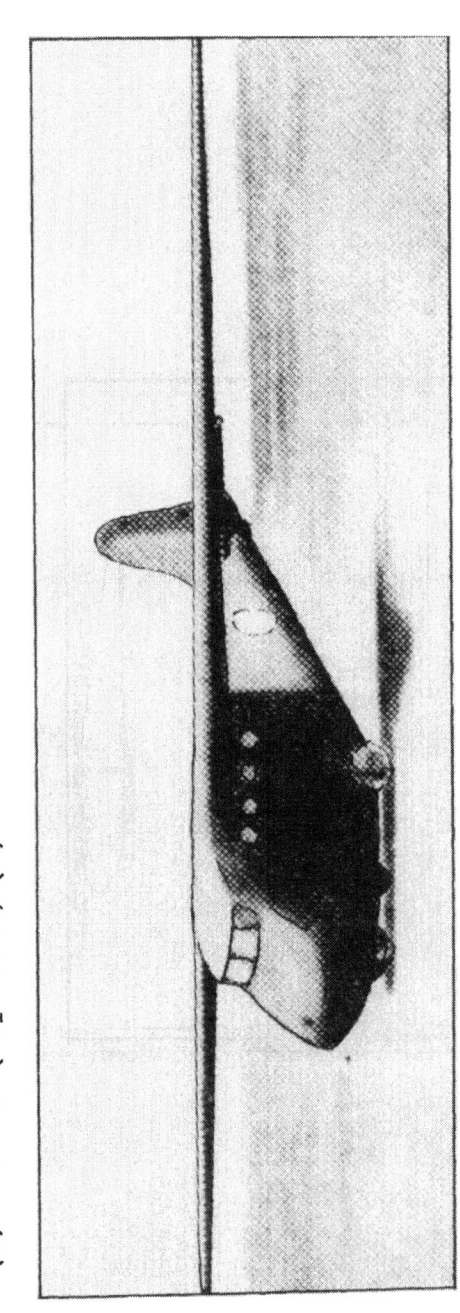

Wing Span :- 54 ft.　Length :- 32 ft.

Military Payload :- 3,000 lbs.　Towing Aircraft :- SAAB-90

Special Features :- Wood and steel tube construction.

Fig. 5　Swedish FL-3 Glider

RESTRICTED

II MILITARY GLIDERS

(a) Gliders (unpowered) (ii)

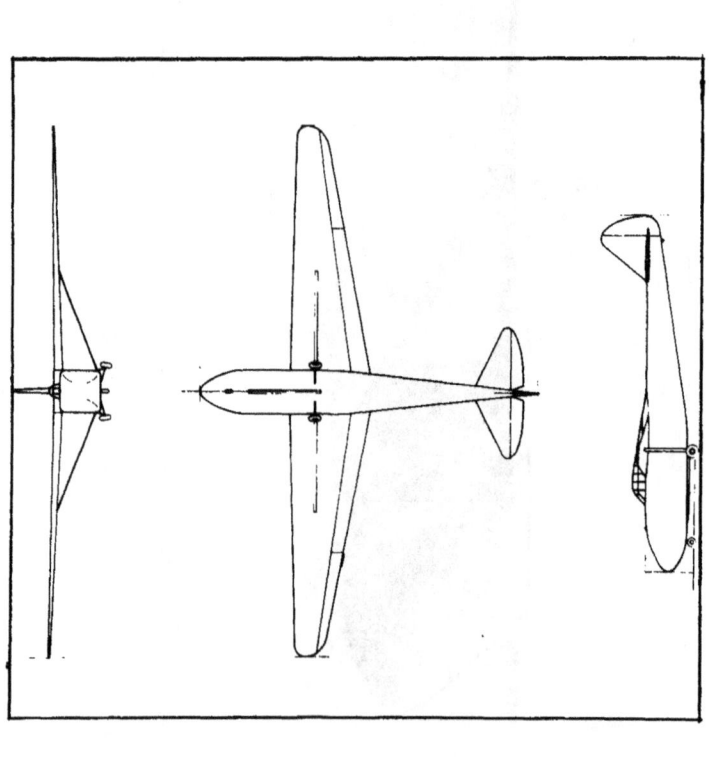

Wing Span :- 80 ft.   Length :- 53½ ft.
Military Payload :- over 2,700 lbs.   Towing Aircraft :- L1-2
Probably Nose loading

Fig. 6   Russian Type 25 Glider

RESTRICTED

II MILITARY GLIDERS

(a) Gliders (unpowered) (ii)

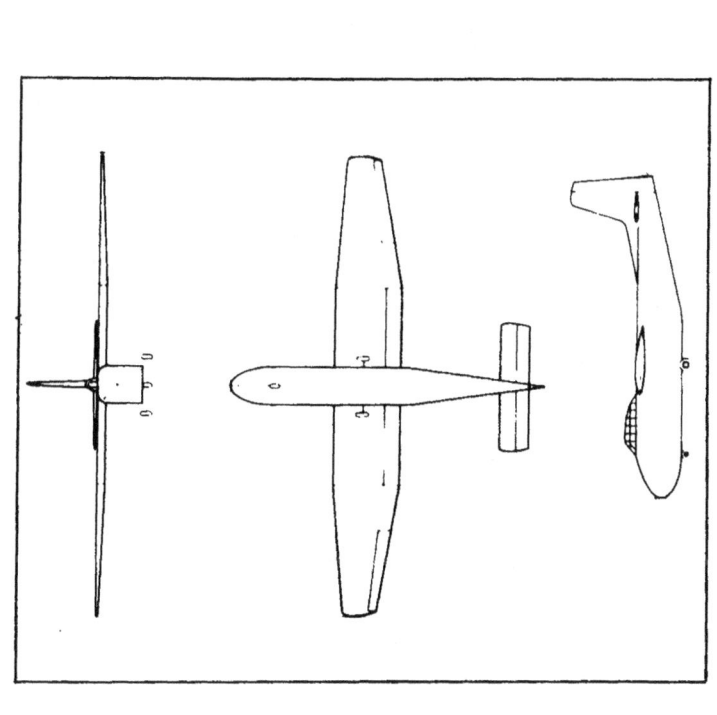

Wing Span :- 85 ft. Length :- 60 ft.
Military Payload :- over 5,200 lbs. Towing Aircraft :- IL-12
Probably Nose loading

Fig. 7 Russian Type 24 Glider

II MILITARY GLIDERS
(a) Gliders (unpowered) (ii)

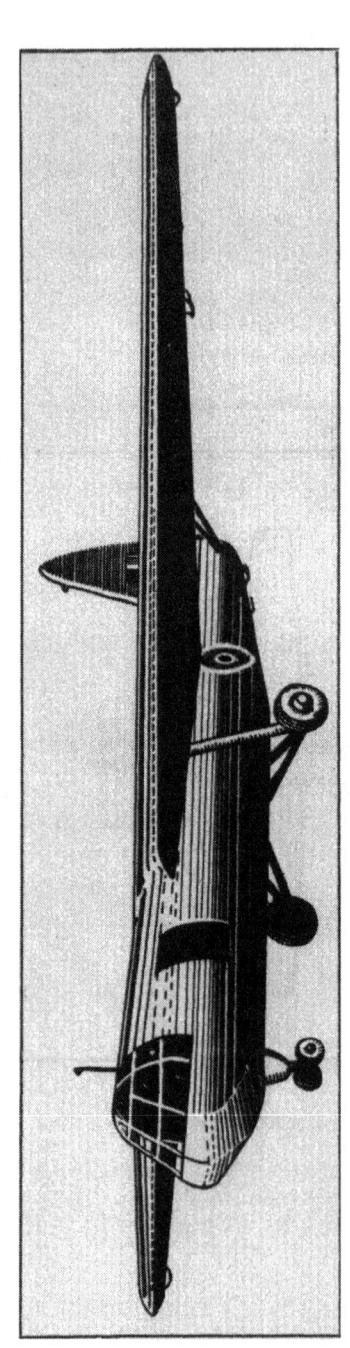

Wing Span :- 88 ft.   Length :- 67 ft.

Military Payload :- 6,900 lbs.   Towing Aircraft :- Dakota

Special Features :- The HORSA II nose hinges to allow nose loading.

Fig. 8   British HORSA I   Medium Glider

RESTRICTED

II   MILITARY GLIDERS

(a) Gliders (unpowered) (ii)

Wing Span :- $84\tfrac{1}{3}$ ft.   Length :- $58\tfrac{1}{2}$ ft.
Military Payload :- 7,720 lbs. Towing Aircraft :- Dakota
Special Features :- Nose loading

Fig. 9   French C.M.10   Medium Glider

II MILITARY GLIDERS

(a) Gliders (unpowered) (ii)

Wing Span :- 110 ft.   Length :- 68 ft.

Military Payload :- 17,800 lbs.   Towing Aircraft :- Halifax

Special Features :- Nose Loading

Fig. 10   British HAMILCAR   Heavy Glider

II MILITARY GLIDERS
(a) Gliders (unpowered) (ii)

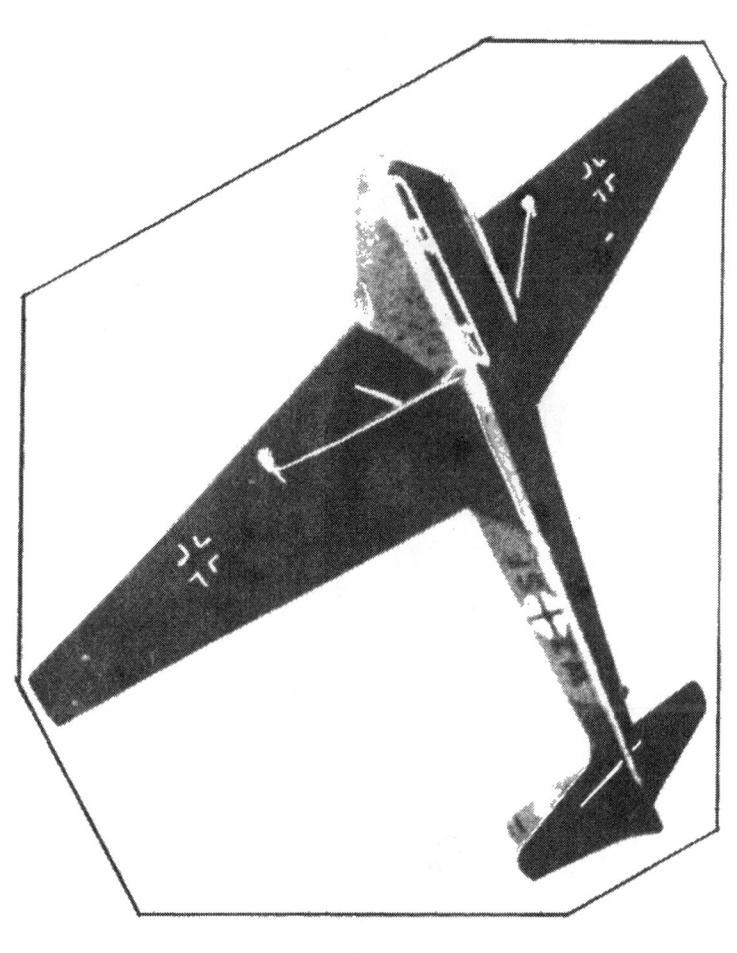

Wing Span :- 180 ft.   Length :- 79 ft.
Military Payload :- 47,000 lbs.   Towing Aircraft :- HE.111 Z.
Special Features :- Clam shaped doors in nose.

Fig. 11   German M.E. 321   (GIGANT)

II MILITARY GLIDERS

(a) Gliders (unpowered) (iii)

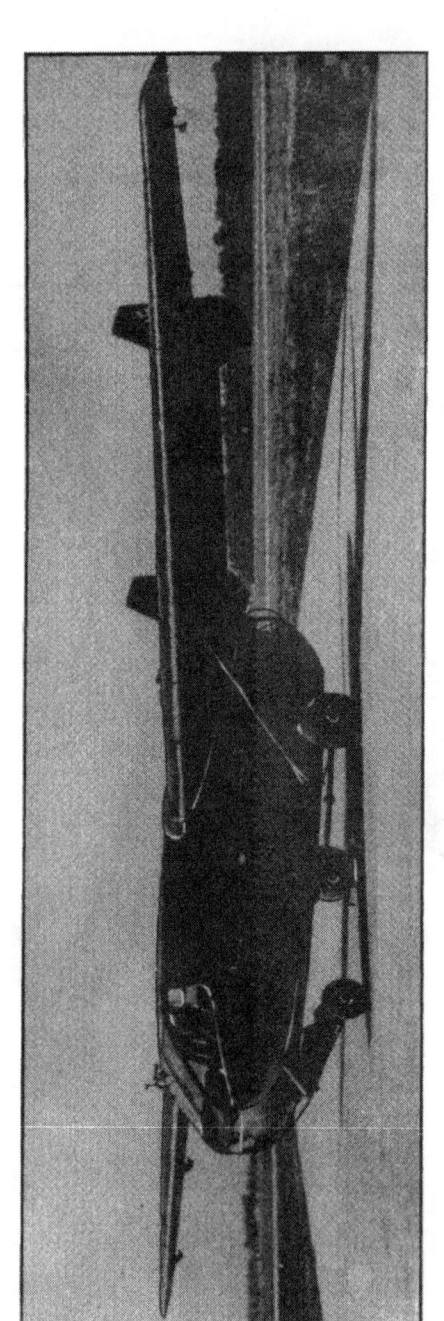

Wing Span :- 79 ft.   Length :- $52\frac{1}{2}$ ft.

Military Payload :- 5,300 lbs.   Towing Aircraft :- JU-52

Special Features :- Tail loading

Fig. 12   German GOTHA 242 Glider

II   MILITARY GLIDERS

(a) Gliders (unpowered) (iii)

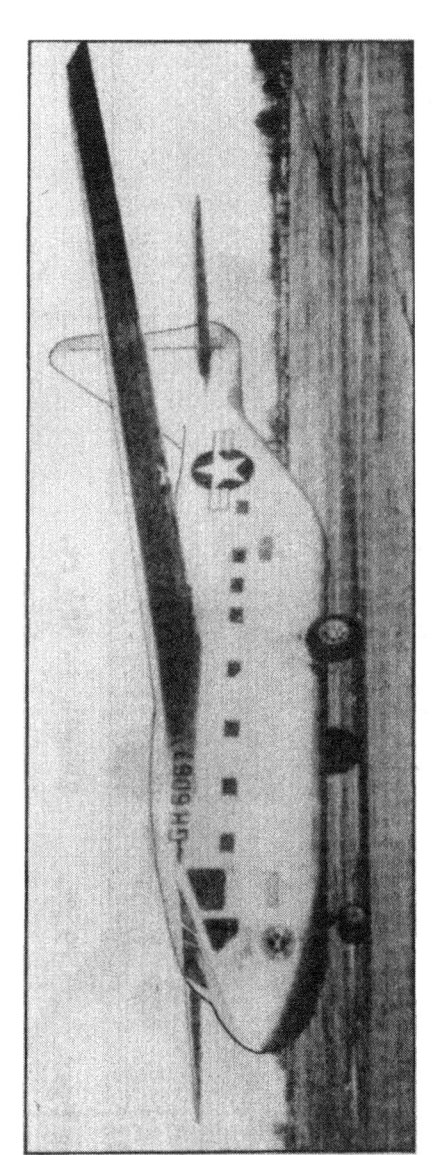

Wing Span :- $86\frac{1}{3}$ ft.   Length :- $53\frac{1}{3}$ ft.

Military Payload :-   over 9,000 lbs.

Special Features :-   Tail loading doors with ramp.

Fig. 13   U.S.A.   Chase XCG-18A   Medium Glider

II MILITARY GLIDERS

(b) Powered Gliders

Wing Span :- 79 ft.   Length :- $52\frac{1}{2}$ ft.

Military Payload :- 4,400 lbs.

Special Features :- When fully loaded requires assistance for take-off. Tail loading

Fig. 14   German GOTHA 244

II MILITARY GLIDERS

(b) Powered Gliders

Wing Span :- 180 ft.   Length :- $92\frac{1}{2}$ ft.
Military Payload :- 21,500 lbs.
Special Features :- Nose loading by double, clam shell doors.
Requires take-off assistance when loaded

Fig. 15   German M.E. 323

II MILITARY GLIDERS
 (b) Powered Gliders

Wing Span :- 110 ft.   Length :- 68 ft.

Military Payload :- 15,700 lbs.

Special Features :- Nose Loading. Requires take-off assistance when loaded.

Fig. 16 British HAMILCAR X Powered Glider

II MILITARY GLIDERS

(b) Powered Gliders

Wing Span :- 110 ft.   Length :- 77 ft.

Military Payload :- approx. 20,000 lbs.

Special Features :- Land and take-off from rough or sandy ground in 600 yds. Tail loading clamshell door with ramp.

Fig. 17 U.S.A. Chase XC-123 (Assault Aircraft)

SECTION III

PARACHUTES

SECTION III   PARACHUTES

(a) Nomenclature and techniques.

    (i) Parachute and parasheet parts and construction.

    (ii) Ripcord parachutes and their auxiliaries.

    (iii) Methods of development of Ripcord and Statichutes.

(b) Parachutes by types.

Many different types of parachutes and parasheets have been developed. This section only attempts to show some of the more popular types which have had military consideration.

    (i) Shaped Gore Parachutes.

    (ii) Flat Gore   "

    (iii) Square and Triangular Parachutes.

    (iv) Lobe Parachutes.

    (v) Blank Gore and paper Parachutes.

    (vi) Ribbon Parachutes.

SECTION III   PARACHUTES

(a)   Nomenclature and techniques

  (i)   Fig 1   Parachute parts
          Fig 2   Gore Shapes and Constructions
          Fig 3   Gathered parasheet
          Fig 4   Ungathered parasheet

  (ii)   Fig 5   Ripcord Parachute - Back type
          Fig 6   Ripcord Parachute - Seat type

  (iii)   Fig 7   Parachute development by Auxiliary 'chute
          Fig 8   Parachute development by static line
          Fig 9   Methods of assisting canopy development
          Fig 10   Parachute deformity - the blown perifery

(b)   Types

  (i)   Fig 11   Shape Gore parachute

  (ii)   Fig 12   British X Type, Flat Gore
          Fig 13   Russian PD-6

  (iii)   Fig 14   Russian Square Aircrew parachute PL-3M
          Fig 15   Russian Square parachute (1949)
          Fig 16   Russian Triangular Parachute (Hofman type)

  (iv)   Fig 17   The Russell lobe parachute
          Fig 18   German Mushroom or Beret Type
          Fig 19   German Guide Surface parachute
          Fig 20   Czech Lobe parachute

  (v)   Fig 21   The Blank Gore parachute
          Fig 22   Russian type with Radical slits
          Fig 23   Swedish NIFO F.60/48 paper type

  (vi)   Fig 24   German WAKO, Tangential, Ribbon parachute
          Fig 25   German, Concentric, Ribbon parachute

III PARACHUTES

(a) Nomenclature and Techniques (i)

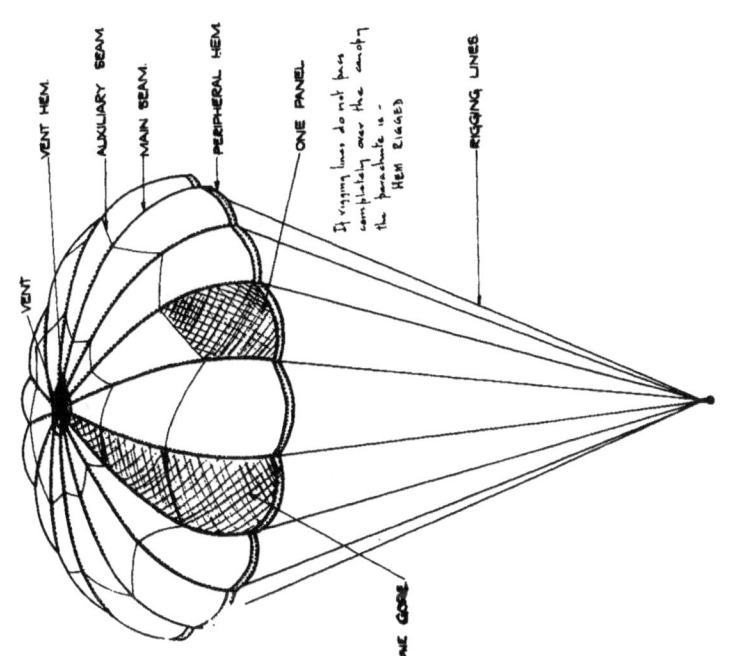

Fig. 1 Parachute Parts

III PARACHUTES

(a) Nomenclature and techniques (i)

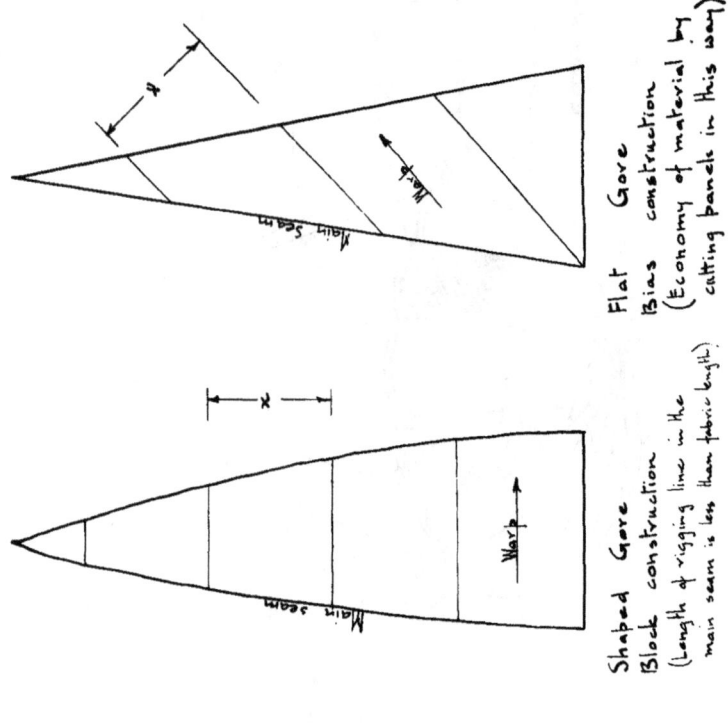

Fig. 2 Gore shapes and constructions

III PARACHUTES
(a) Nomenclature and Techniques (i)

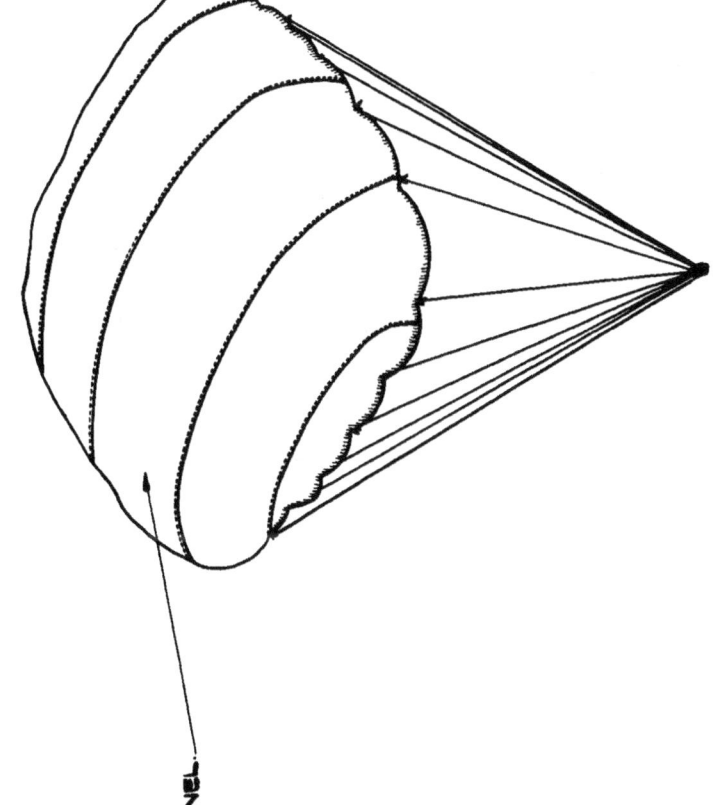

PANEL

Fig. 3 Gathered Parasheet

III/4

III PARACHUTES
(a) Nomenclature and Techniques (i)

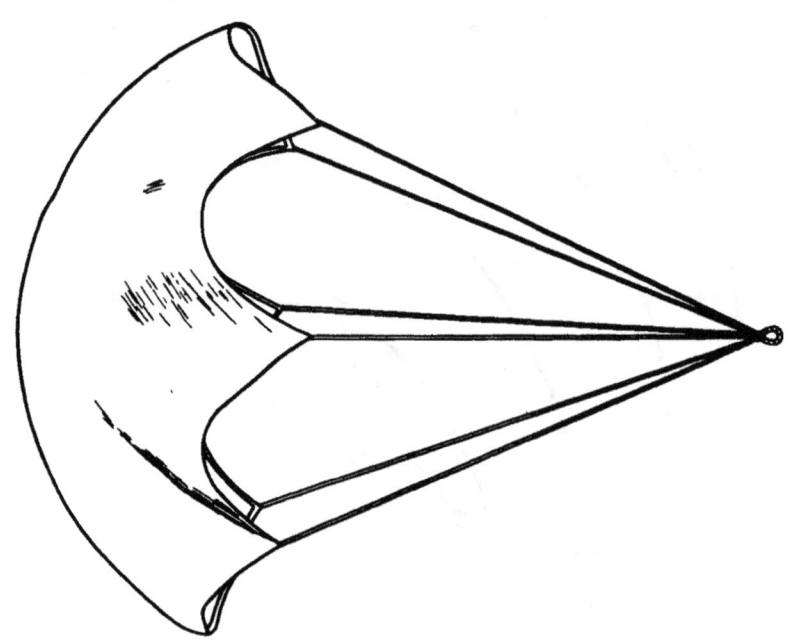

Fig. 4 Ungathered Parasheet

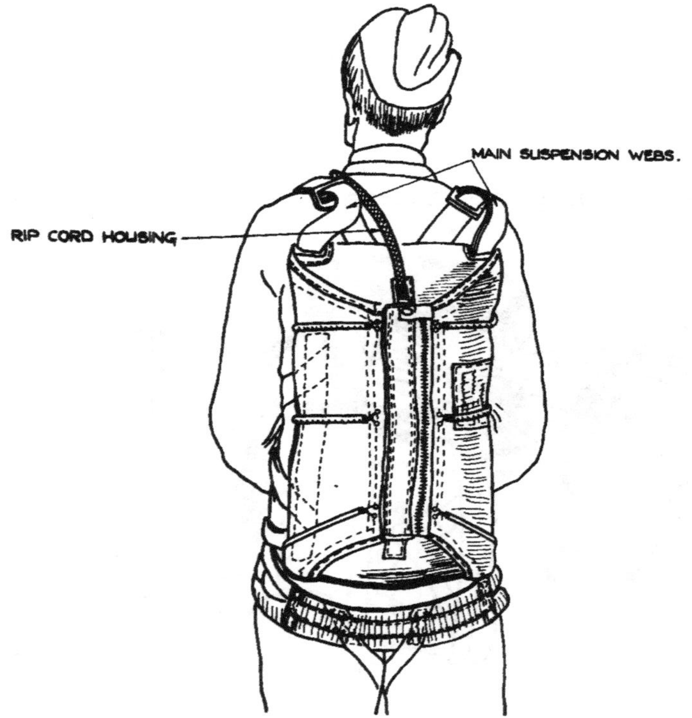

III   PARACHUTES
(a)   Nomenclature and techniques (ii)

Fig. 5   Ripcord Parachute - Back type

III/5

III PARACHUTES
(a) Nomenclature and techniques (ii)

The Auxiliary parachute is often spring loaded so that opens automatically as it is released from the pack

Fig. 6   Ripcord Seat Type Parachute

III PARACHUTES
(a) Nomenclature and Techniques (iii)

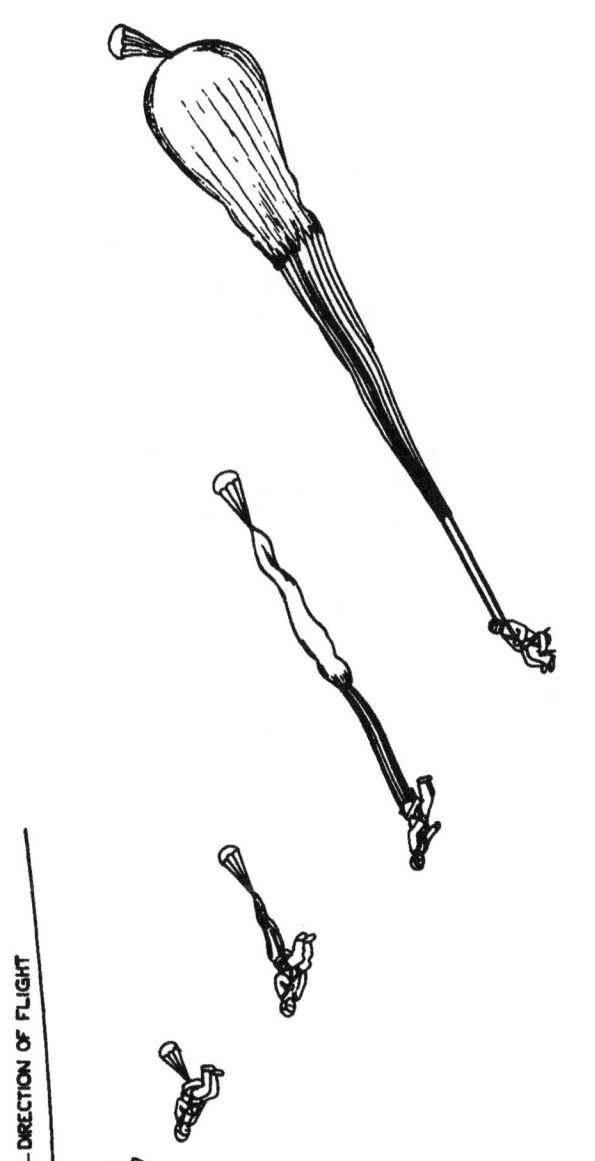

Fig. 7   Parachute development by Auxiliary 'chute

III PARACHUTES
(a) Nomenclature and Techniques (iii)

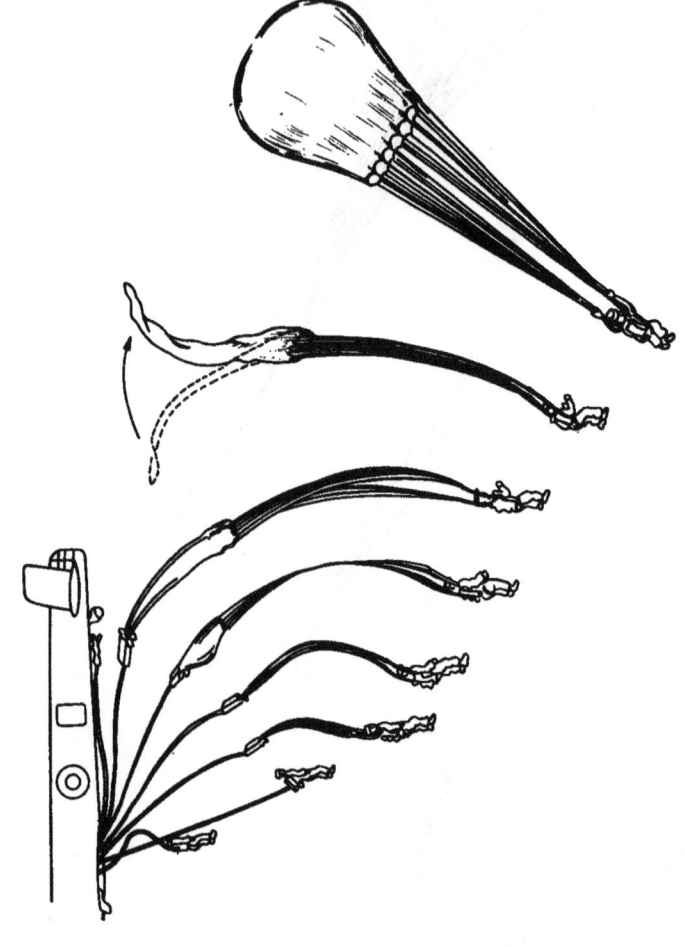

A line attached to the aircraft withdraws the pack from the parachute in place of the ripcord and auxiliary parachute.

Fig 8   Parachute development by static line

III PARACHUTES
(a) Nomenclature and techniques (iii)

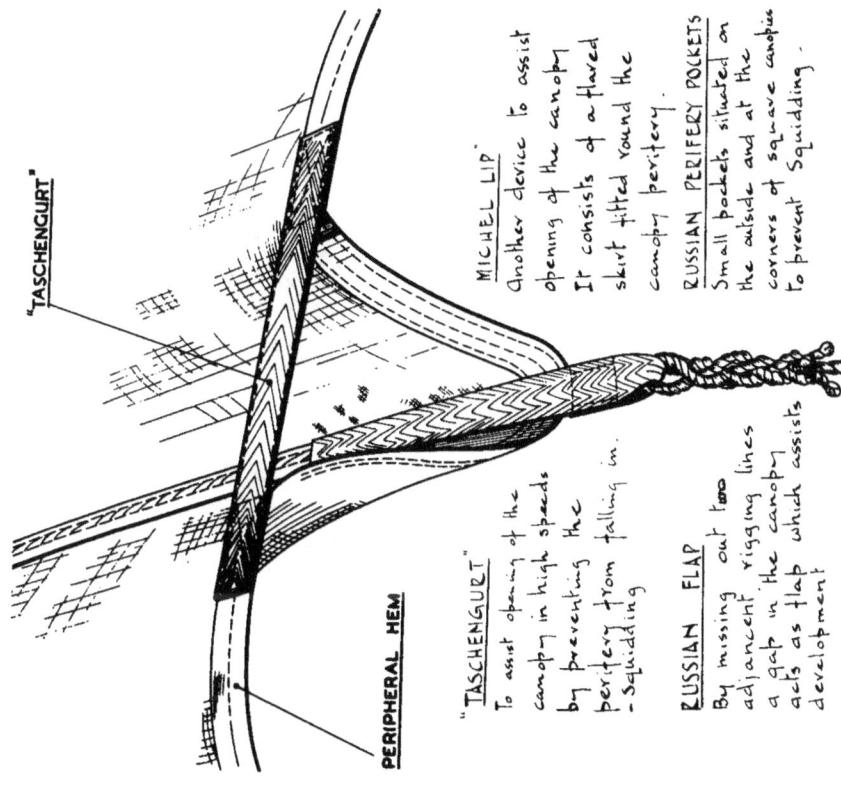

Fig. 9   Methods of assisting canopy development

III/10

III PARACHUTES
(a) Nomenclatures and techniques (iii)

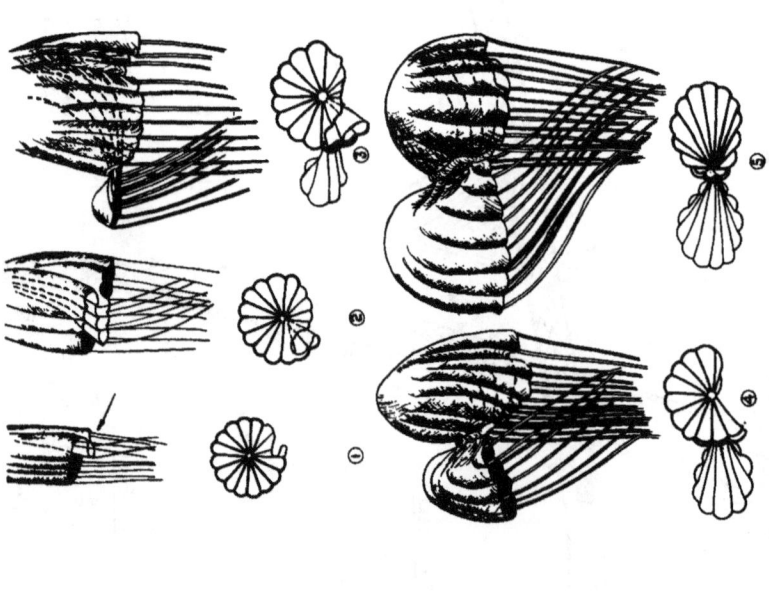

Fig. 10 Parachute deformity - The Blown periphery

III PARACHUTES
(b) Types (i)

Fig. 11 Shaped Gore parachute

III/12

III PARACHUTES
(b) Types (ii)

Fig. 12   Flat Gore type
British X Type Parachute

III PARACHUTES
(b) Types (ii)

III/13

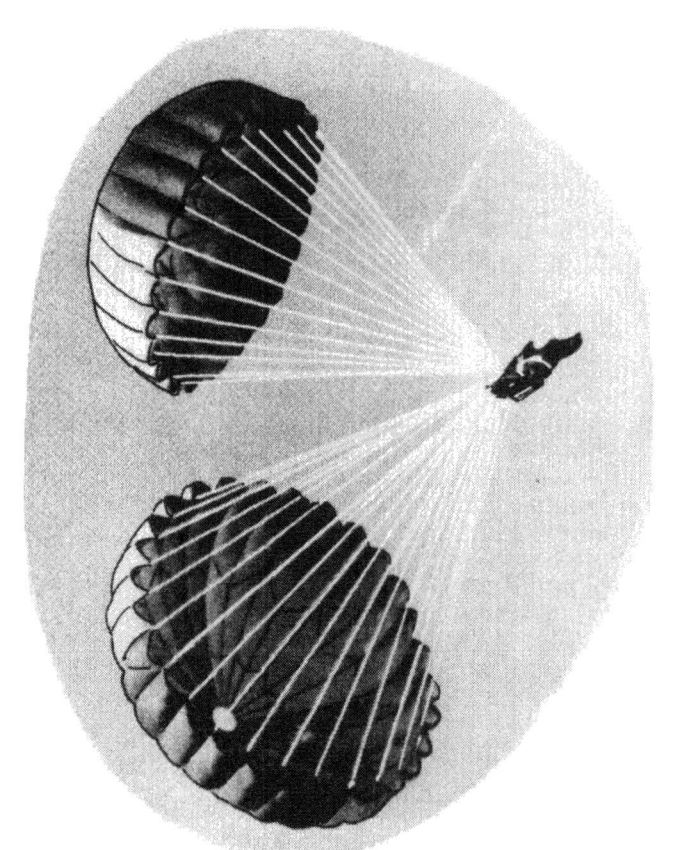

Fig. 13   Russian PD-6 Parachute

RESTRICTED

III PARACHUTES

(b) Types (iii)

Diameter:- 22 ft. square

Fig. 14   Russian square aircrew parachute PL-3M

III/15

III PARACHUTES
(b) Types (iii)

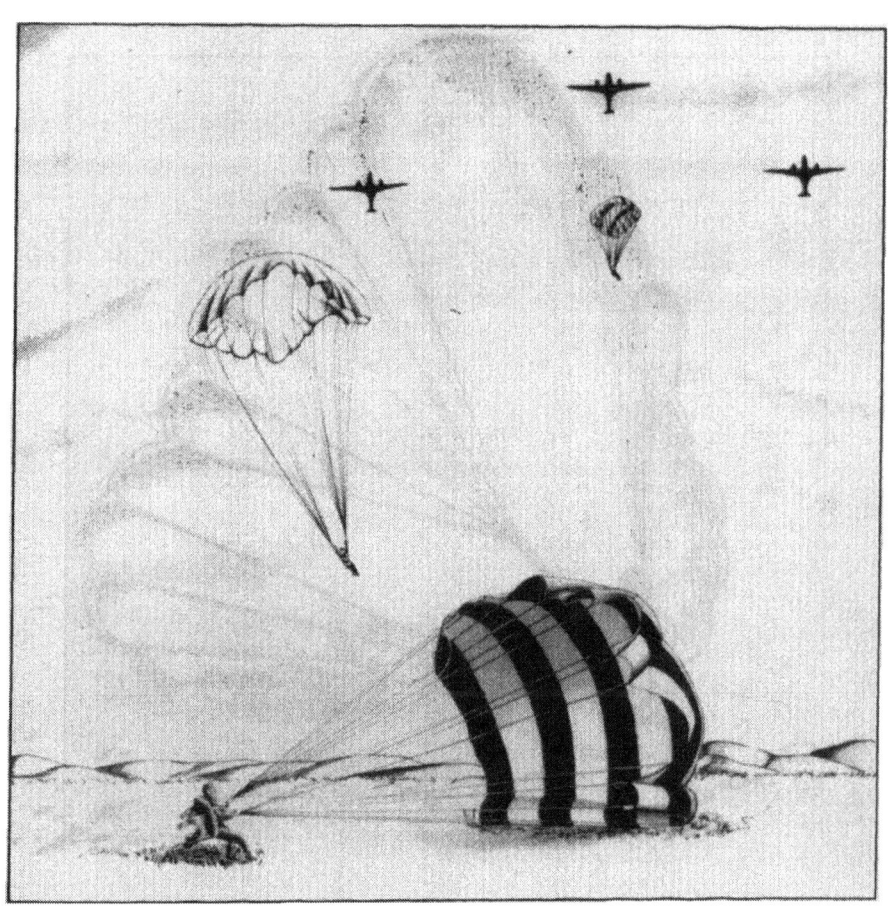

Fig. 15   Russian Square Parachute (1949)

III PARACHUTES
(b) Types (iii)

Fig. 16   Russian Triangular Parachute (Hofman Type)

III   PARACHUTES
(b) Types (iv)

The lobe makes the parachute very stable

Fig. 17   The Russell lobe Parachute

III/18

III   PARACHUTES
(b)   Types (iv)

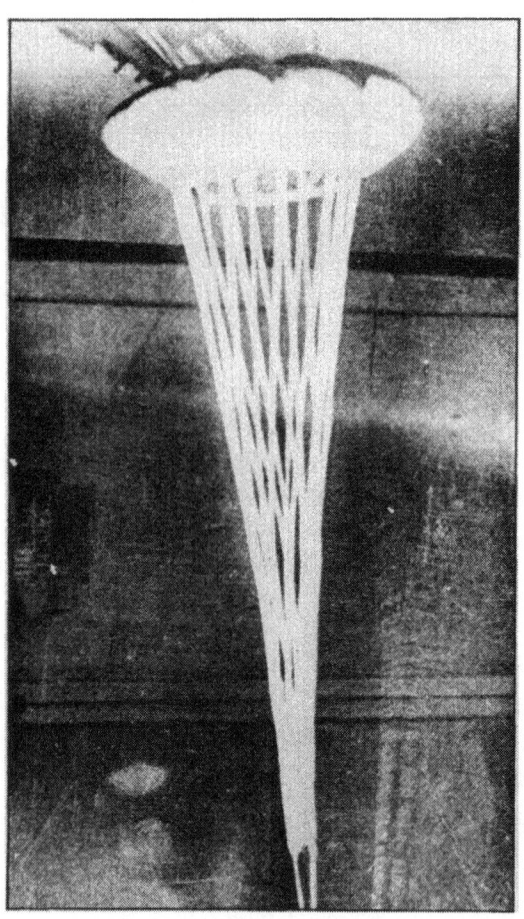

Special Features :- The Criss-Crossing of the rigging lines is to reduce the tendency of the load to rotate.

Fig. 18   German Mushroom or Beret Type Parachute

III   PARACHUTES

(b)   Types (iv)

This parachute combines the attributes of the "Michel Lip" (easy opening) and lobe parachute (stability)

Fig. 19   German Guide Surface Parachute

III   PARACHUTES
(b)   Types (iv)

Note:- Similarity is German Guide Surface Parachute

Fig. 20   Czech lobe parachute

III/21

III   PARACHUTES

(b)   Types (v)

A very stable parachute

Fig. 21   The Blank Gore Parachute

III   PARACHUTES

(b)   Types (v)

Fig. 22   Russian Parachute with Radial Slits

III   PARACHUTES   III/23

(b)   Types (v)

Diameter:-   approx. 14 ft.

Vents on the perifery of the canopy increase stability. Larger ones are also manufactured.

Fig. 23   Swedish NIFO F 60/48   Paper Parachute

III   PARACHUTES

(b)   Types (vi)

Porosity of fabric increasing from base to apex to facilitate canopy development at high speeds.

Fig. 24   German "Wako", Tangential Type, Ribbon Parachute

III   PARACHUTES

(b)   Types (vi)

III/25

Fig. 25   German, Concentric type, Ribbon Parachute

SECTION IV

HARNESS/CLOTHING

SECTION IV   PARACHUTING HARNESS AND CLOTHING

- (a) Harnesses and Fastenings
    - (i) Harnesses with multi point fastenings.
    - (ii) Harnesses with single point fastening - Quick release.
- (b) Parachute Clothing and personnel valises
    - (i) Carrying weapons without the use of valises.
    - (ii) Weapon valises, packs and kitbags.

SECTION IV — PARACHUTING HARNESS AND CLOTHING

(a) Harness and Fastenings

  (i)   Fig 1   Russian Paratrooper harness
           Fig 2   German early type harness
           Fig 3   German four point, quick release, harness
           Fig 4   German seat type harness
           Fig 5   Italian parachute harness

  (ii)   Fig 6   French EFA type 675 parachute harness
           Fig 7   Russian seat type parachute Harness (1947)
           Fig 8   French Aerazur 671-672 parachute harness
           Fig 9   British Quick release Box

(b) Clothing and personnel valises

  (i)   Fig 10   A British Method of Weapon (PIAT) carrying
           Fig 11   A Russian Method of Weapon carrying

  (ii)   Fig 12   Japanese weapon case
           Fig 13   British universal valise
           Fig 14   British Kitbag

IV/1

IV PARACHUTING HARNESS AND CLOTHING

(a) Harnesses and Fastenings (i)

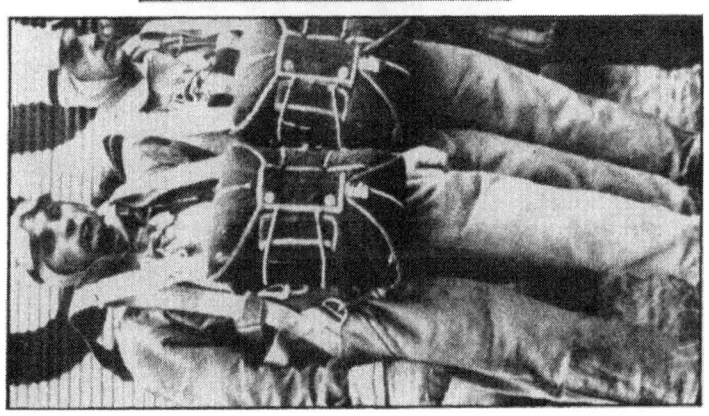

Fig. 1   Russian Paratrooper Harness

IV PARACHUTEING HARNESS AND CLOTHING

(a) Harnesses and fastenings (i)

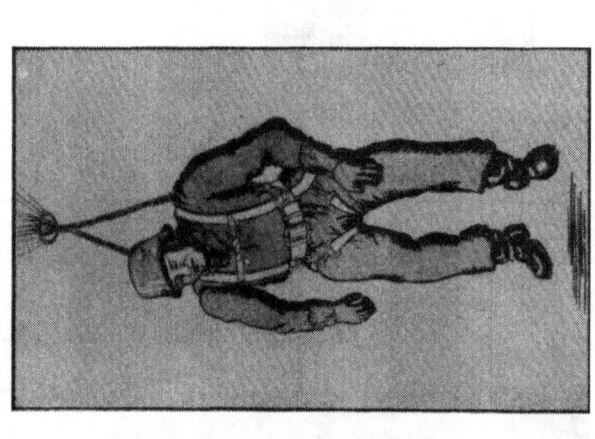

N.B. Rigging lines gathered at a single Point

Fig. 2   Early German Parachute harness

IV/3

IV PARACHUTING HARNESS AND CLOTHING
(a) Harnesses and Fastenings (i)

Fig. 3   German four point, Quick release, Harness

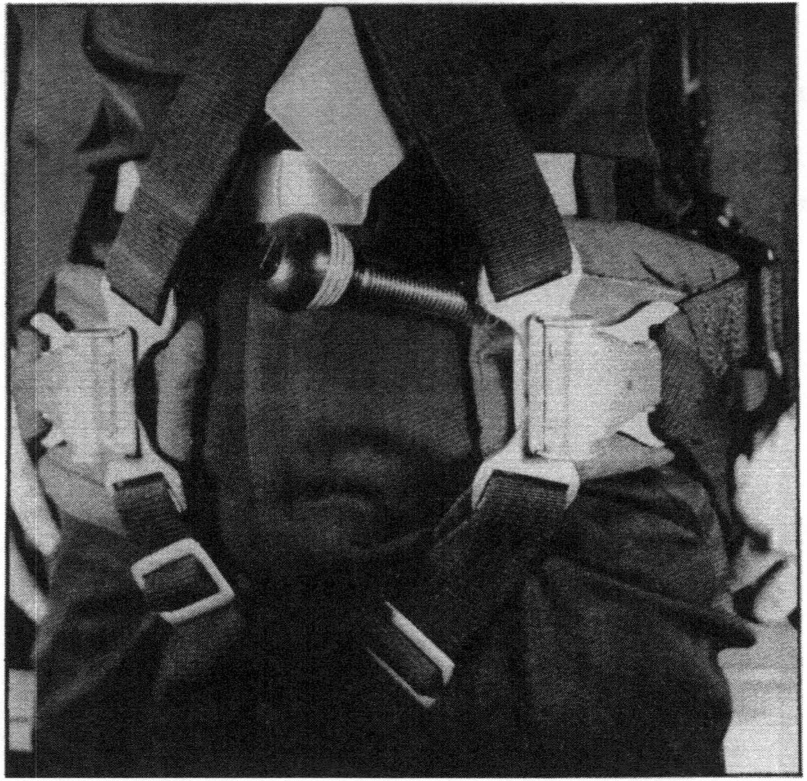

IV/4

IV PARACHUTING HARNESS AND CLOTHING
(a) Harnesses and Fastenings (i)

Fig. 4   German Harness for Ripcord, seat type parachute

IV PARACHUTING HARNESS AND CLOTHING

(a) Harnesses and Fastenings (i)

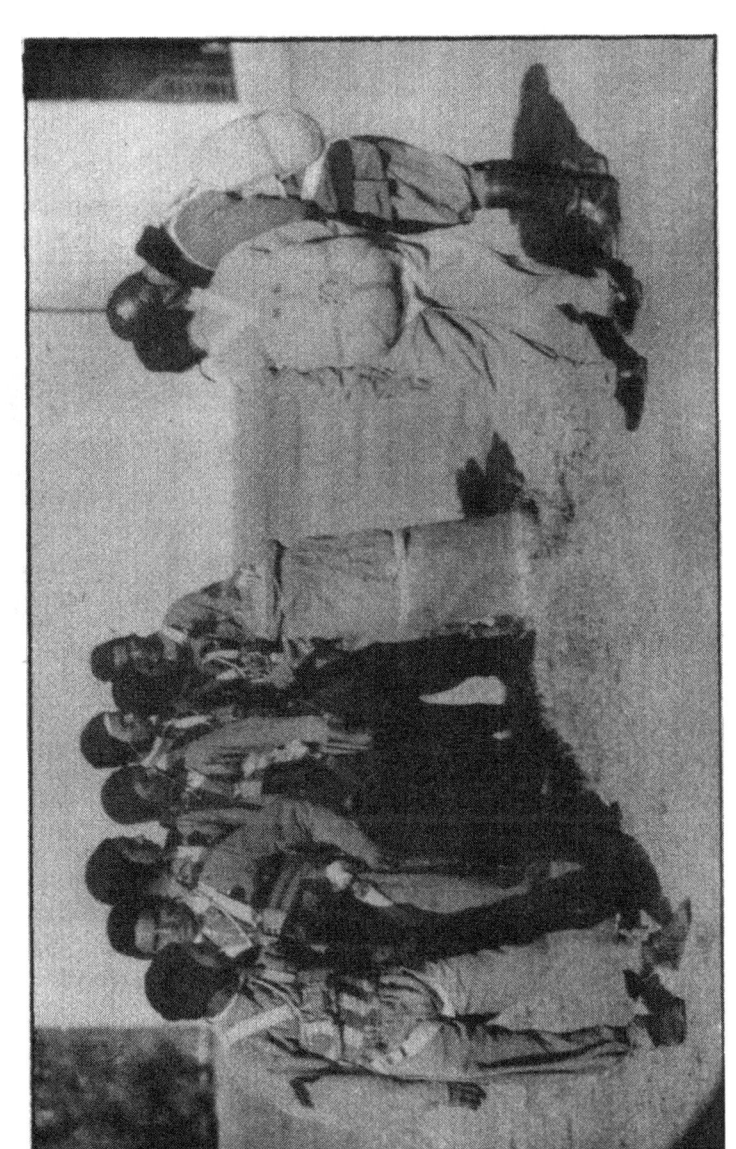

Fig. 5   Italian Parachute Harness

RESTRICTED

IV PARACHUTE HARNESS AND CLOTHING
(a) Harnesses and Fastenings (ii)

Fig. 6   French E.F.A. Type 675 Parachute Harness

RESTRICTED

IV/7

IV PARACHUTING HARNESS AND CLOTHING

(a) Harnesses and Fastenings (ii)

Fig. 7   Russian seat type parachute Harness (1947)

IV PARACHUTE HARNESS AND CLOTHING

(a) Harnesses and Fastenings (ii)

(a) with reverse parachute
(b) without reverse parachute

Fig. 8   French Aerazur 671-672 Parachute Harness

IV/9

IV   PARACHUTING HARNESS AND CLOTHING

(a)   Harnesses and Fastenings (ii)

Fig. 9   British Quick release Box

IV   PARACHUTING HARNESS AND CLOTHING

(b) Clothing and personnel valises (i)

Fig. 10   British Method of weapon (P.I.A.T.) carrying

IV PARACHUTING HARNESS AND CLOTHING

(b) Clothing and personnel valises (i)

Machine Carbine with folding stock
Leather Helmet and Grey overalls

Fig. 11 A Russian method of weapon carrying

IV/12

IV PARACHUTE HARNESS AND CLOTHING
(a) Clothing and personnel valises (ii)

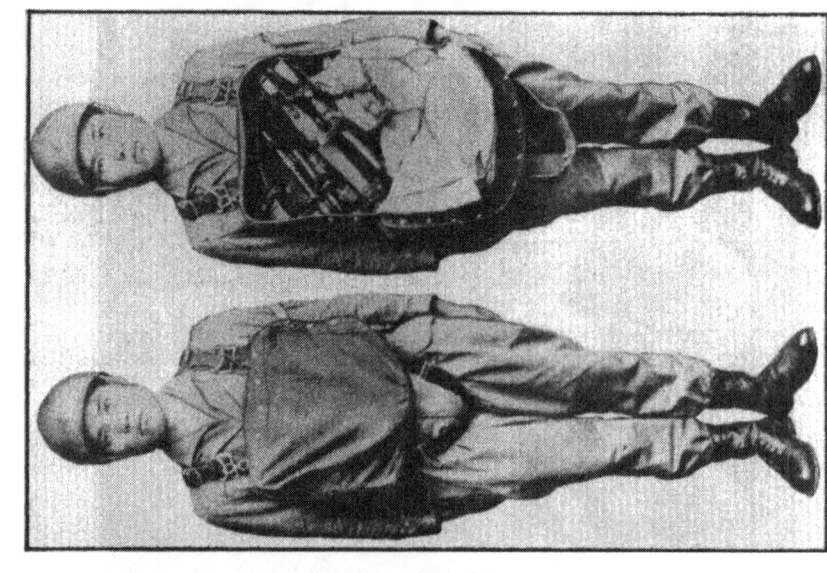

Fig. 12　Japanese Weapon Case

IV/13

IV PARACHUTING HARNESS AND CLOTHING

(b) Clothing and personnel valises (ii)

(a) with weapon valise
(b) Stomach bag only

Fig. 13   British Universal Valise

IV/14

IV   PARACHUTING HARNESS AND CLOTHING

(b) Clothing and personnel Valises (ii)

Fig. 14   British Kitbag

SECTION V

CONTAINERS

SECTION V — AIRBORNE CONTAINERS

(i) Improvised containers, stores cradles and harnesses.

(ii) Canvas, wickerwork and fibre containers.

(iii) Metal containers.

(iv) Trolley containers (detachable stub axle wheels).

(v) Airborne trolleys.

(vi) Airborne bicycles.

(vii) Container locating devices.

SECTION V   AIRBORNE CONTAINERS

(i)   Fig 1   Improvised Russian Container
         Fig 2   British Mk VI stores Harness
         Fig 3   British Cradle type L for stores

(ii)   Fig 4   Russian Old pattern canvas container
         Fig 5   British SEAC canvas pack
         Fig 6   British Airborne Pannier (wicker basket)
         Fig 7   Two panniers prepared for "Daisy-chain" drop
         Fig 8   British Collapsible Pannier
         Fig 9   Japanese Fibre container

(iii)   Fig 10   British F type container
         Fig 11   British CLE Mk. 1 container
         Fig 12   U.S.A. container on Monorail
         Fig 13   Obsolete Russian containers
         Fig 14   Russian stores container PDMM
         Fig 15   Russian Liquid container PDBB
         Fig 16   German Three man container
         Fig 17   German 1000 Kg. container
         Fig 18   German Composite Supply container
         Fig 19   German liquid container

(iv)   Fig 20   German Mobile container
         Fig 21   German container for mines
         Fig 22   German container for Air Compressor

(v)   Fig 23   German Airborne trailer
         Fig 24   British Airborne trolley
         Fig 25   U.S.A. Handcart

(vi)   Fig 26   German Folding bicycle container
         Fig 27   Italian Folding bicycle

(vii)   Fig 28   British container Location device

V AIRBORNE CONTAINERS (i)

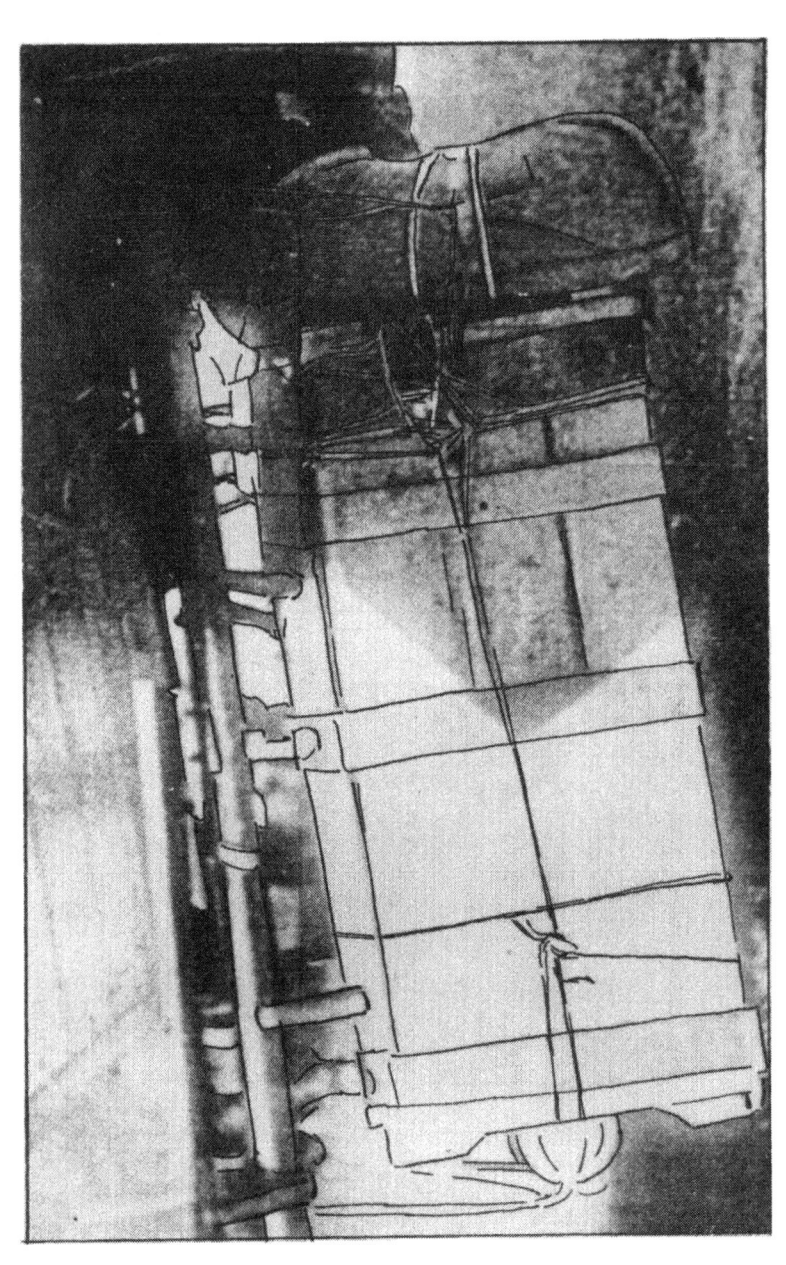

Fig. 1   Improvised Russian Container

V AIRBORNE CONTAINERS (i)

Fig. 2   British Mk. VI Stores Harness

V AIRBORNE CONTAINERS (i)

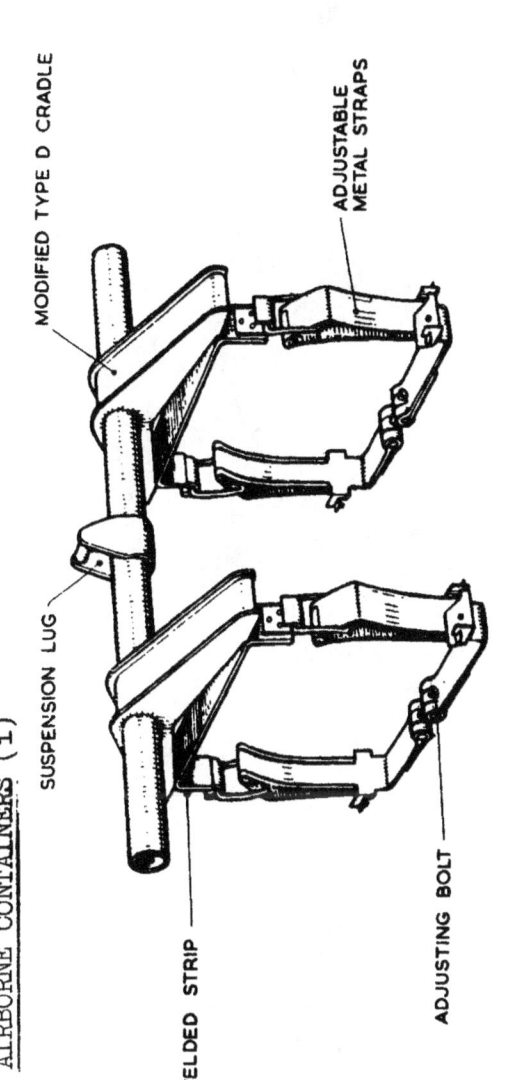
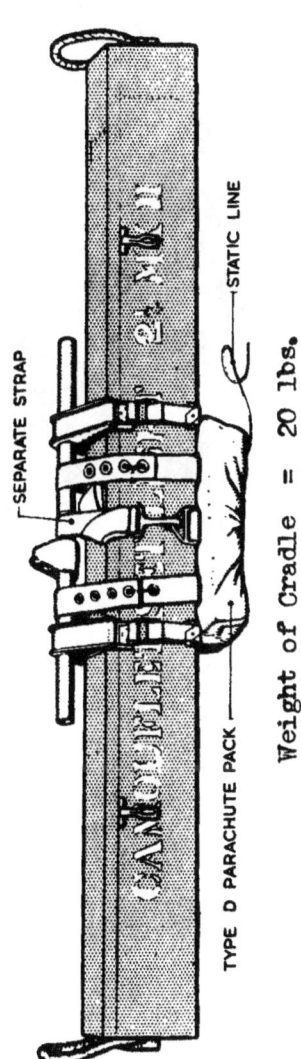

Fig. 3   British Cradle Type "L" for stores

V AIRBORNE CONTAINERS (ii)

Fig. 4   Old Pattern Russian Canvas Weapons Container

V   AIRBORNE CONTAINERS (ii)

Dimensions :-   approx. 3½ ft. high x 1½ ft. square
Load :-   approx. 2000 lbs.
A Sawdust packing piece in the base of the pack softens the landing shock

Fig. 5   British S.E.A.C. Canvas Pack

V   AIRBORNE CONTAINERS (ii)

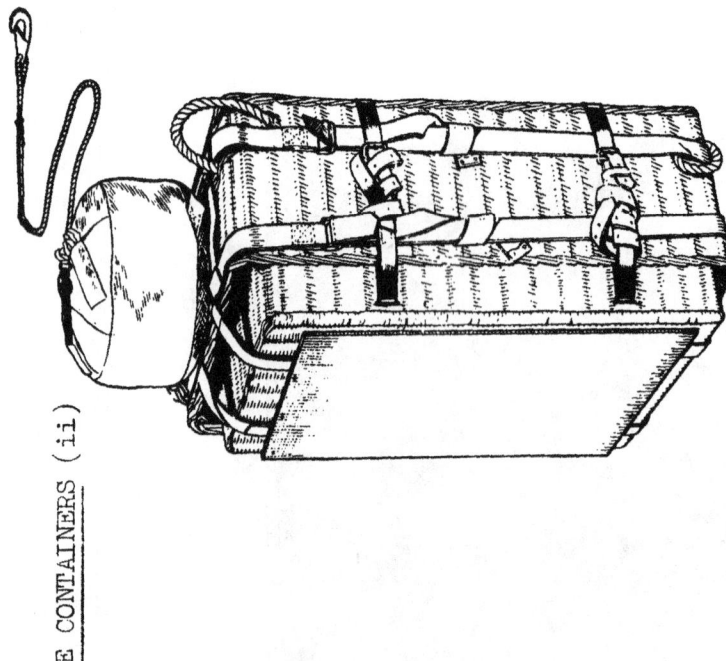

Dimensions :- 36 inches x 20 inches x 16 inches deep

Load :- 350 lbs.

Special Features :- The pannier is in two halves and can be expanded to a depth of 30 inches.
The Plywood base is for use with roller conveyor.

Fig. 6   British Airborne pannier (wicker basket)

V   AIRBORNE CONTAINERS (ii)

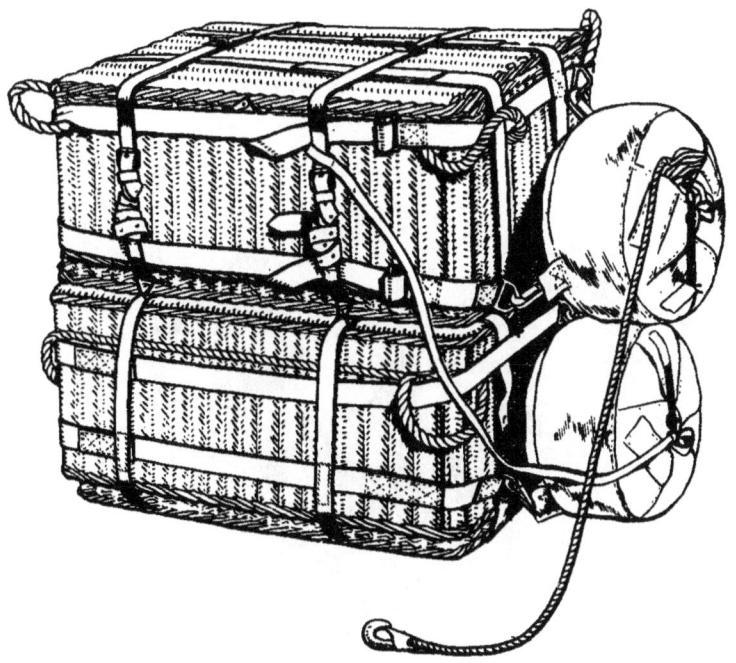

Special Features :-   Two panniers are tied together with
four (100 lb.) ties.   The static line of the top pannier
parachute is attached to the aircraft and that of the bottom
one to the top pannier.   As the fall of the panniers is
checked by the opening of the top one's parachute the bottom
one breaks away to the **limit** of its static line which operates
its parachute.

Fig. 7   Two panniers prepared for "Daisy-Chain" dropping

RESTRICTED   V/8

V AIRBORNE CONTAINERS (ii)

Dimensions :-   3 ft. long x 2 ft. square (approx.)

Load :-   4000 lbs. (approx.)

Special Features :- Note quick release tapes on side straps.

Fig. 8   British Collapsible Pannier

V   AIRBORNE CONTAINERS (ii)

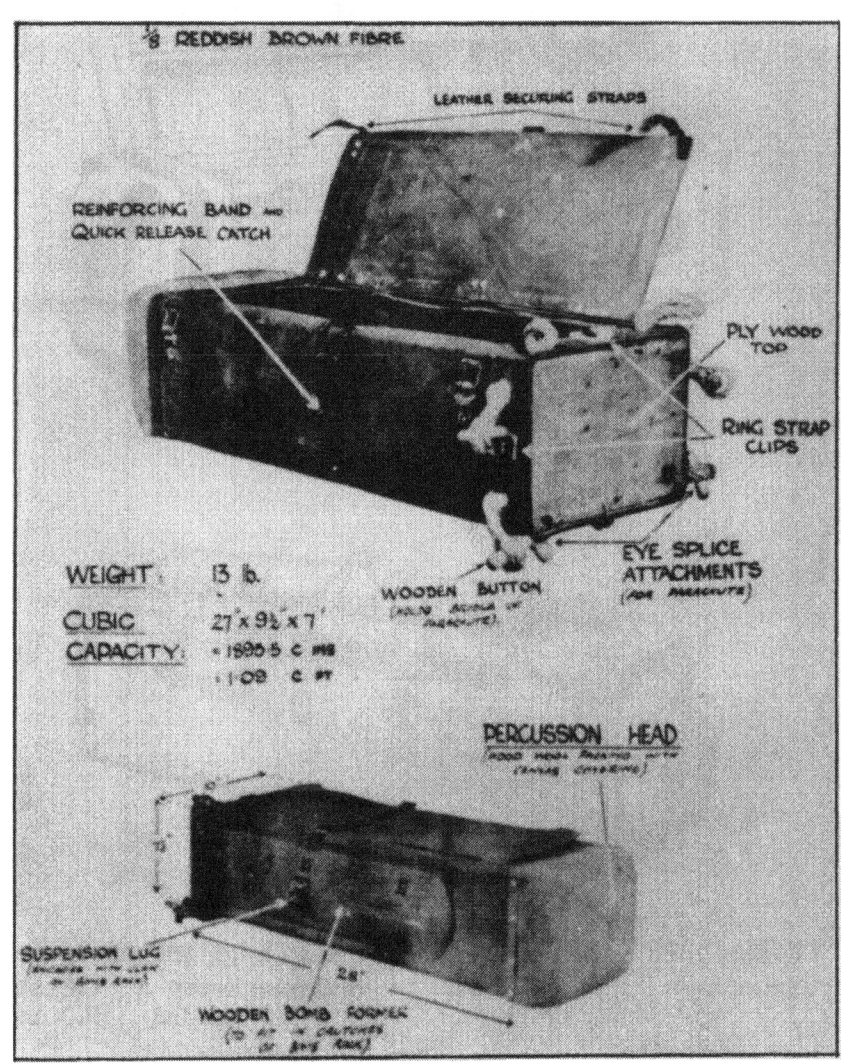

Fig. 9   Japanese Fibre Container

V   AIRBORNE CONTAINERS (iii)

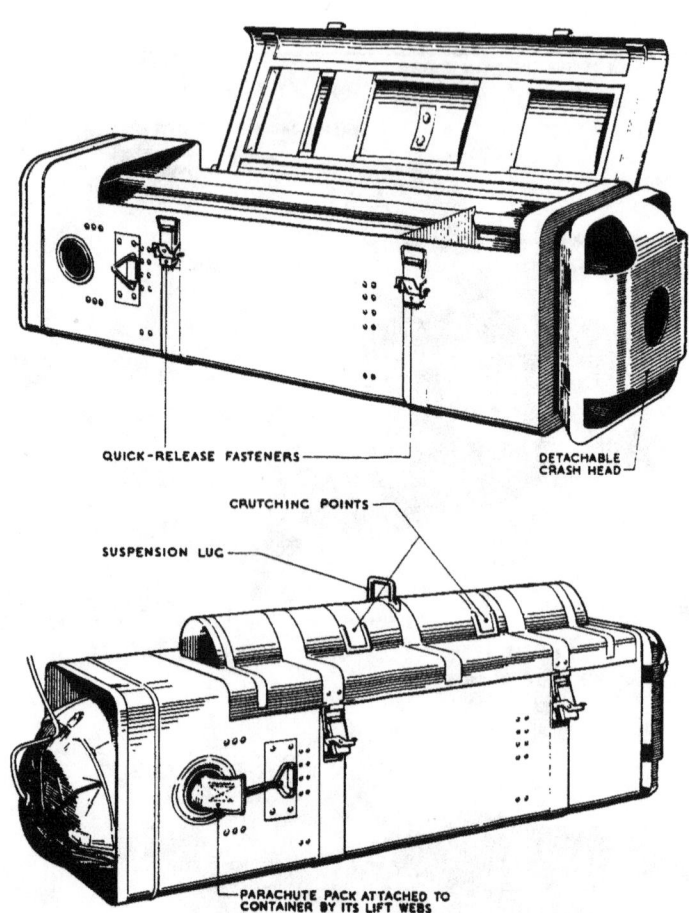

```
Dimensions :-      approx. 5 ft. long x 15 inches square
Load :-            200 lbs.      Weight:- Empty    132 lbs.
                                          Loaded   340 lbs.
Special Features :-   No Cradle required
```

Fig. 10   British Type F Container

V AIRBORNE CONTAINERS (ii)

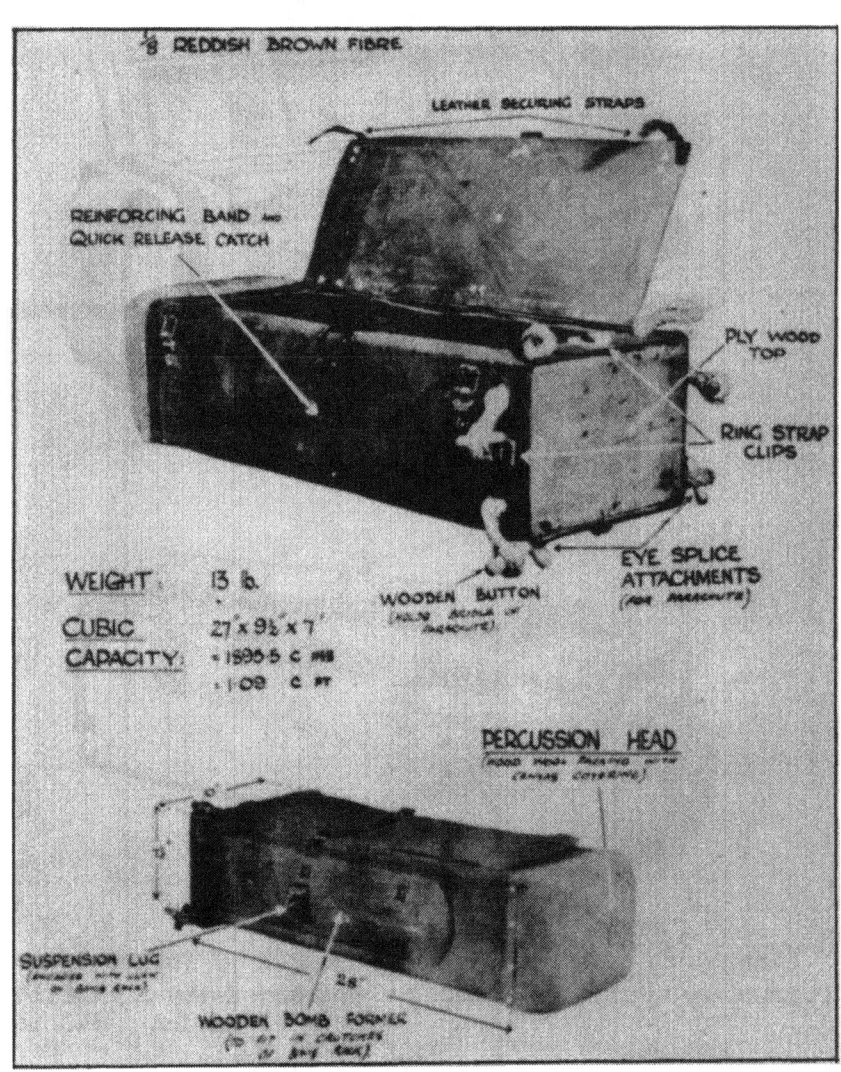

Fig. 9   Japanese Fibre Container

V AIRBORNE CONTAINERS (iii)

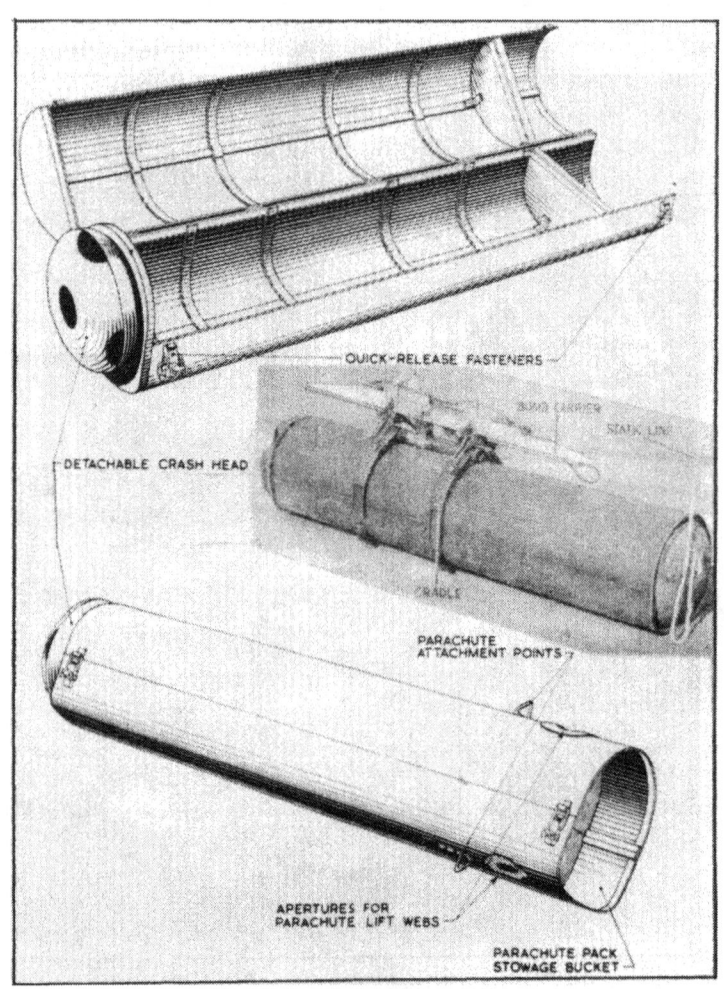

Dimensions :- (approx.) 6 ft. long x 15 inches diameter
Load :-   300 - 400 lbs. Weight Empty = 110 lbs.
                           Weight loaded = up to 500 lbs.

Fig. 11   British CLE Mk. 1 Container

RESTRICTED   V/12

V   AIRBORNE CONTAINERS (iii)

   The Containers are loaded on the Fairchild Packet
monorail and are dropped through a hatch towards the front
of the Aircraft.

        Fig. 12   U.S.A. Container on Monorail

V   AIRBORNE CONTAINERS (iii)

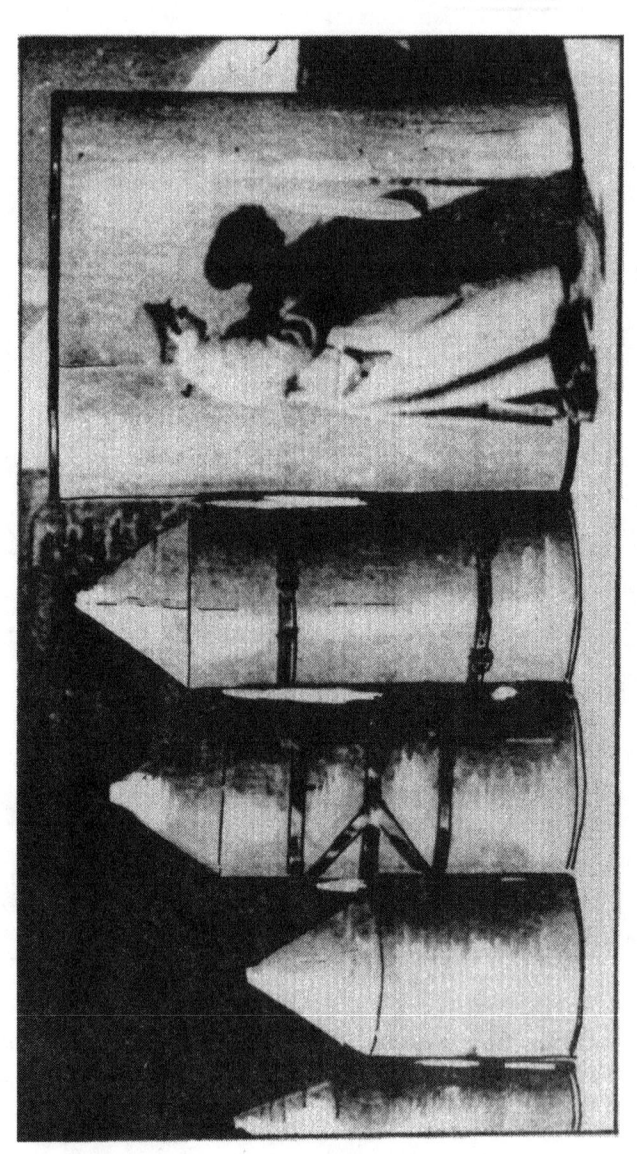

Fig. 13   Some Obsolete Russian Containers

RESTRICTED

V   AIRBORNE CONTAINERS (iii)

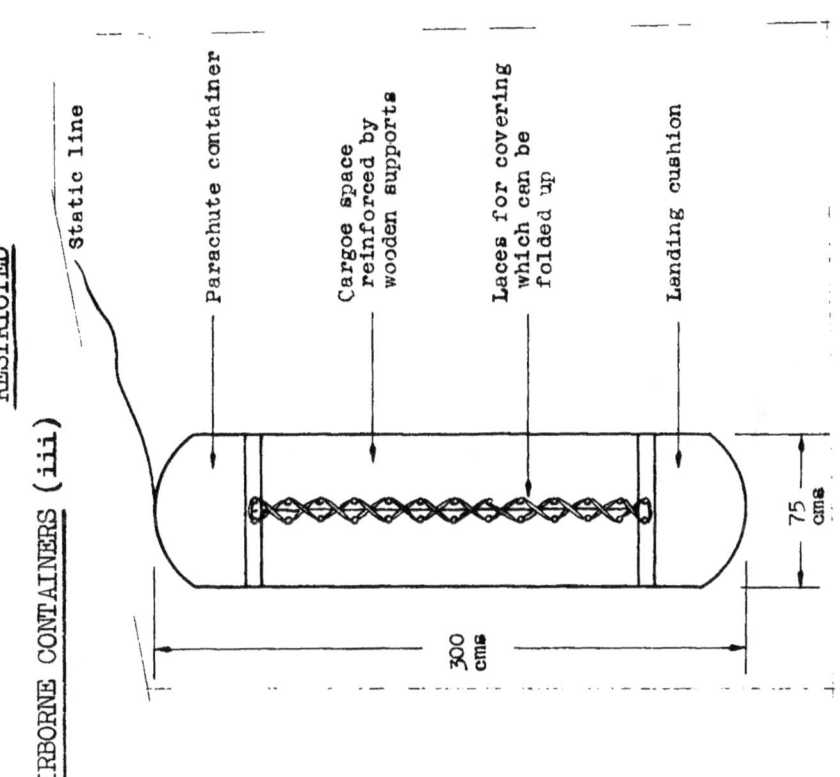

Load :-   Weapons up to about 200 lbs.

Fig. 14   Russian Stores Container PDMM

V AIRBORNE CONTAINERS (iii)   RESTRICTED

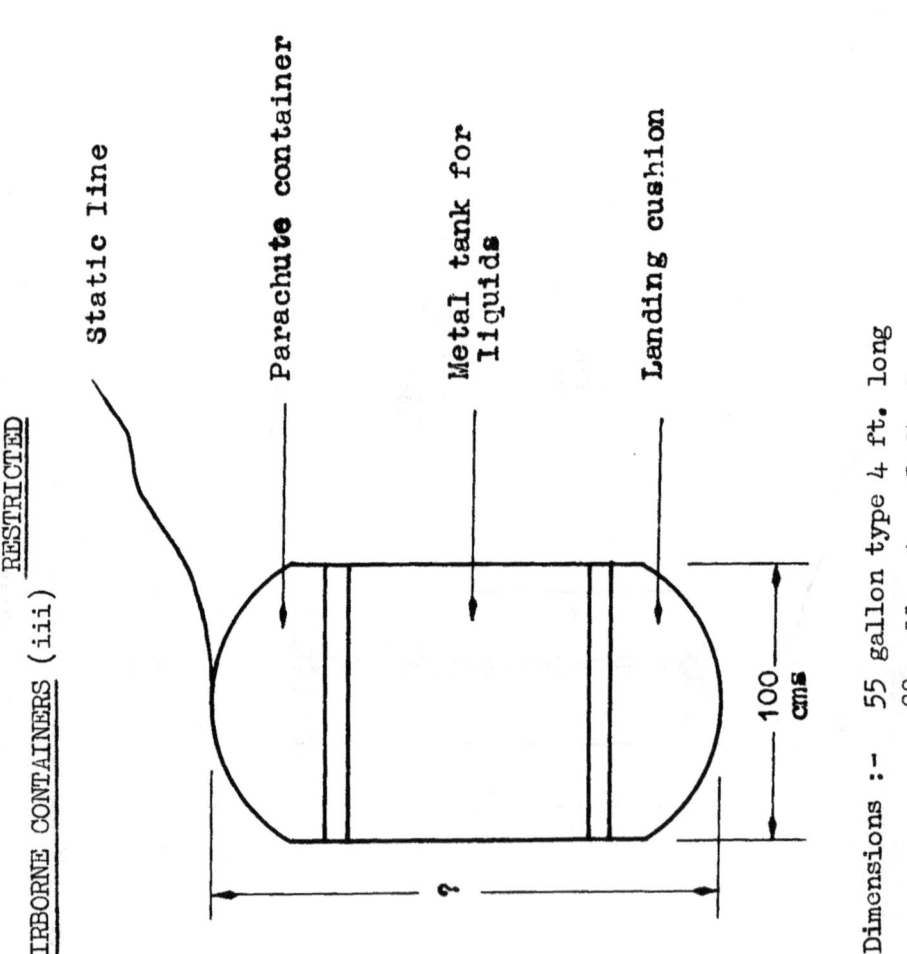

Dimensions :- 55 gallon type 4 ft. long
              88 gallon type 5 ft. long

Fig. 15   Russian Liquid Container PDBB

V AIRBORNE CONTAINERS (iii)

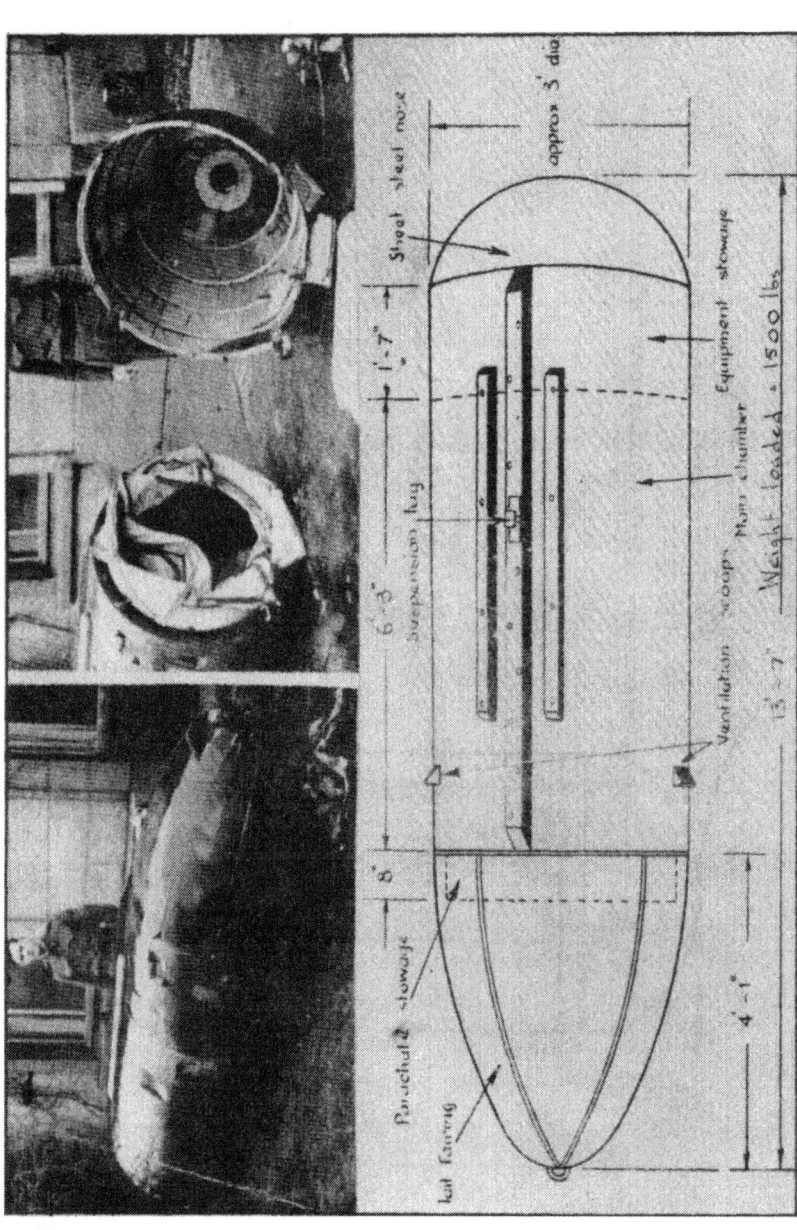

Special Features :- Used for dropping agents
Fig. 16 German three man Container

V AIRBORNE CONTAINERS (iii)

(1) Parachute compartment
(2) Parachute delay opening device
(3) Locking handle
(4) Load compartment
(5) Suspension points
(6) Percussion head

Weight of container :-

Loaded = 2,150 lbs.
Empty =   620 lbs.
Overall Length = 10.4 ft.
Diameter   = 26 inches

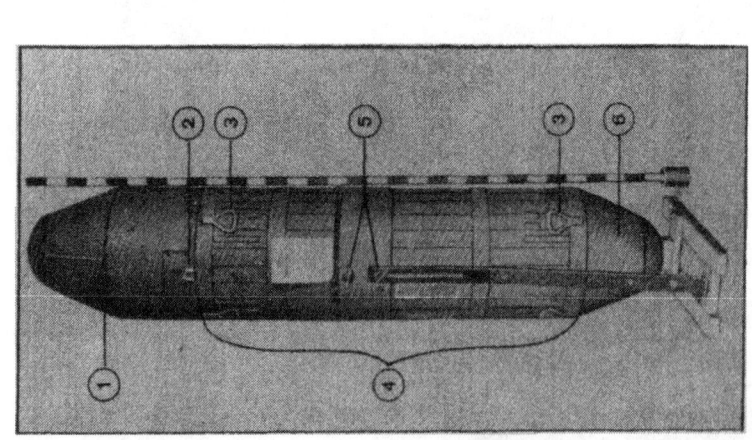

Fig. 17   German 1000 Kg. Container

V   AIRBORNE CONTAINERS (iii)

Fig. 18   German Composite Supply Container

V AIRBORNE CONTAINERS (iii)

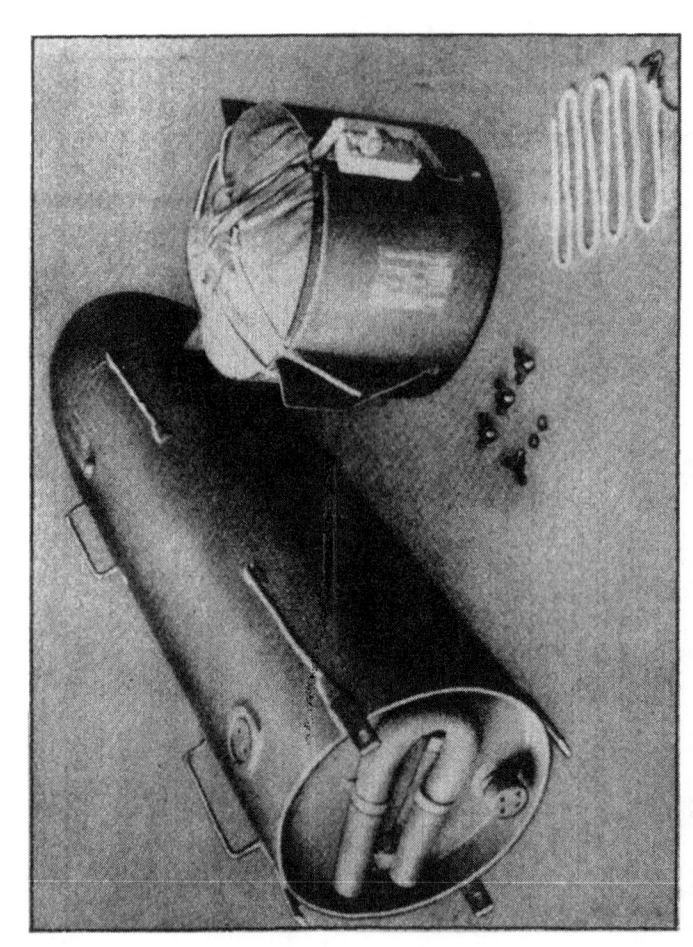

Load :- 24 gallons
Weight Empty = 121 lbs.
Weight Full = 330 lbs.

Length = $5\frac{1}{2}$ ft.   Diameter = 15 inches

Fig. 19 German liquid Container

V AIRBORNE CONTAINERS (iv)

Light metal percussion head fitted

Handle and stub axle wheels stowed inside container

Weight empty 100-120 lbs

Parachute pack

3 types

	Length	Section
Mobile Weapon Container long	5' 2"	15" square
Mobile Weapon Container short	4' 6"	15" square
Mobile Multi purpose container	4' 6"	15" square

Fig. 20 German Mobile Container

V   AIRBORNE CONTAINERS (iv)

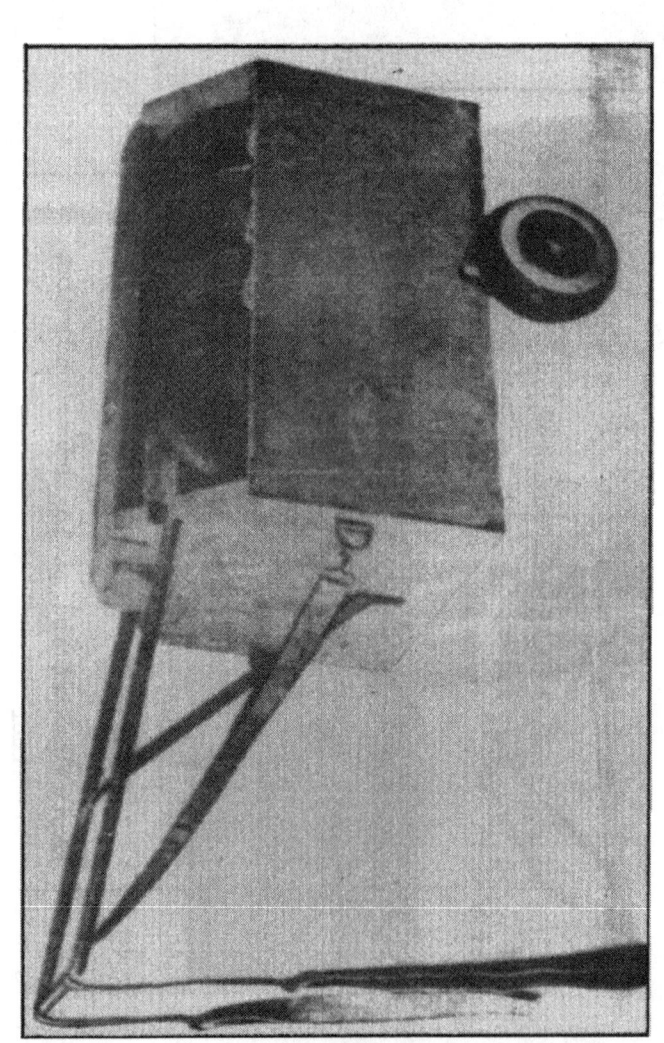

Load :- Empty = 154 lbs., Loaded = 390 lbs.
Special Features :- Handle and stub axle wheels stowed internally.

Fig. 21   German Container for Mines

V   AIRBORNE CONTAINERS (iv)

Load :-   Empty = 184 lbs., loaded = 580 lbs.

Special Features :- Handle and stub axle wheels stowed internally.

Fig. 22   German Container for Air Compressor

V   AIRBORNE CONTAINERS (v)

Fig. 23   German Airborne Trailer

V   AIRBORNE CONTAINERS (v)

Fig. 24   British Airborne Trolley

RESTRICTED

V AIRBORNE CONTAINERS (v)

The Trolley can be lifted easily by one person and may be towed at speed by a vehicle.

Fig. 25   U.S.A. Handcart

V   AIRBORNE CONTAINERS (vi)

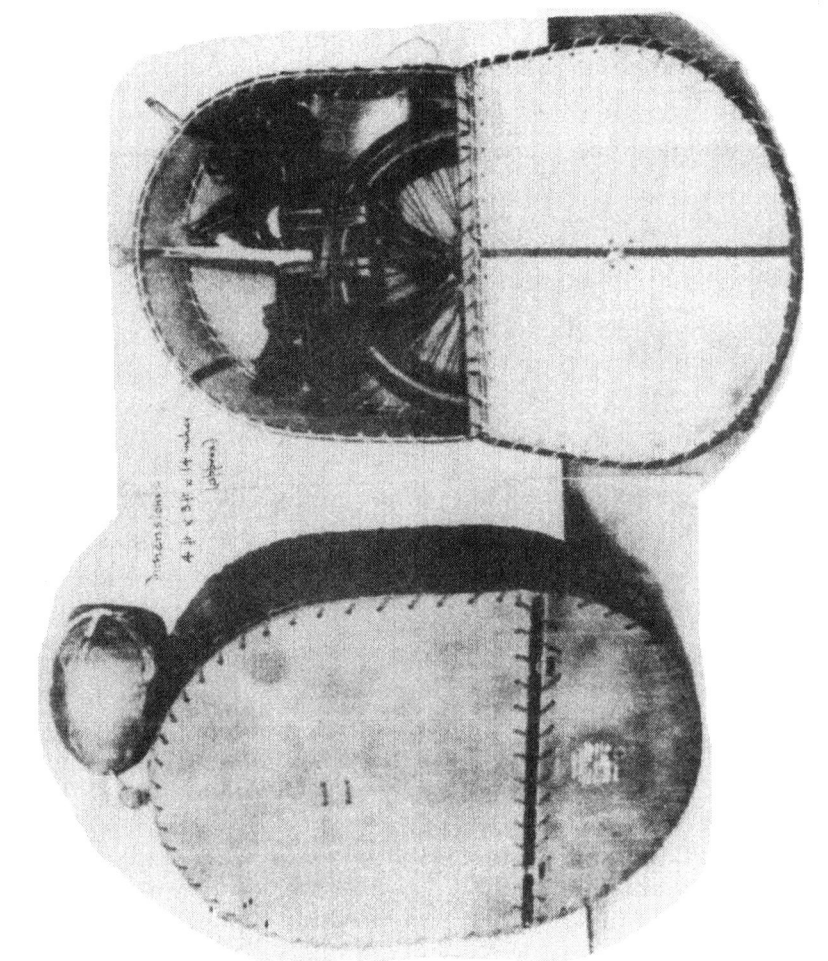

Weight Loaded = 110 lbs.
Fig. 26   German Folding bicycle Container

V   AIRBORNE CONTAINERS (vi)

Fig. 27   Italian Folding Bicycle

V   AIRBORNE CONTAINERS (vii)

Dimensions :- approx. 6 ft. high

Special Features :- Housed in a tube fitted to the container.
It is ejected from the tube by the development of the
parachute and remains attached to the Container by a line.

Fig. 28   British Container Location device

SECTION VI

HEAVY DROPPING

SECTION VI — HEAVY DROPPING TECHNIQUES

(i) Early Russian methods.

(ii) Steel frame crating gears.

(iii) Crash pans and parachute ground release devices.

(iv) Suspension gear.

(v) Pallets and Skid Boards.

(vi) Roller conveyors for stores in aircraft.

(vii) Pallet ejection methods.

(viii) Paratechnicon dropping.

(ix) Heavy dropping parachute development methods.

(x) Heavy drop parachutes and methods of load attachment.

SECTION VI   HEAVY DROPPING TECHNIQUES

INDEX

(i)   Fig 1   Russian Obsolete Personnel vehicle
      Fig 2   Russian Obsolete Equipment vehicle
      Fig 3   Russian Crating gear for two m/c sidecars

(ii) Fig 4   German Crating gear for 3.7 cm A Tk. Gun
      Fig 5   German 10.5 cm Recoilless Gun, Crating gear

(iii) Fig 6   British Lt. Wt. Trailer Crated for dropping
      Fig 7   A parachute ground release device (Heavy drop:)
      Fig 8   Another parachute ground release device

(iv) Fig 9   Jeep and Gun in bomb bay of HALIFAX
      Fig 10   Heavy dropping Beam for HASTINGS
      Fig 11   German heavy dropping suspension Gear for JU-52.
      Fig 12   German 2 c.m. AA Gun prepared for dropping
      Fig 13   German M/c sidecar prepared for dropping

(v)   Fig 14   British Pallet for heavy dropping
      Fig 15   15 cwt Truck loaded on pallet
      Fig 16   U.S.A. AA Gun on Pallet (Skid Board)

(vi) Fig 17   U.S.A. Roller conveyor for PACKET
      Fig 18   British Roller conveyor for HASTINGS

(vii) Fig 19   Pallet discharge by Gravity
      Fig 20   Pallet discharge by ejector parachute

(viii) Fig 21 British paratechnicon

(ix) Fig 22   A Standard British method of Heavy Dropping
      Fig 23   Russian Heavy dropping (Pre 1939)

(x)   Fig 24   Russian 130 ft dia. parachute (Pre 1939)
      Fig 25   Cluster of twelve 32 ft flat parachutes
      Fig 26   Cluster of four 60 ft flat parachutes
      Fig 27   Example of parachutes splitting
      Fig 28   U.S.A. 100 ft dia. parachutes

VI HEAVY DROPPING TECHNIQUES (i)

This equipment containing four or five men was free dropped from low flying aircraft and skidded along the ground.

Fig. 1   Russian Obsolete Personnel vehicle

VI HEAVY DROPPING TECHNIQUES (i)

Landed by same means as Personnel Vehicle

Fig. 2 Russian obsolete equipment vehicle

VI HEAVY DROPPING TECHNIQUES (i)

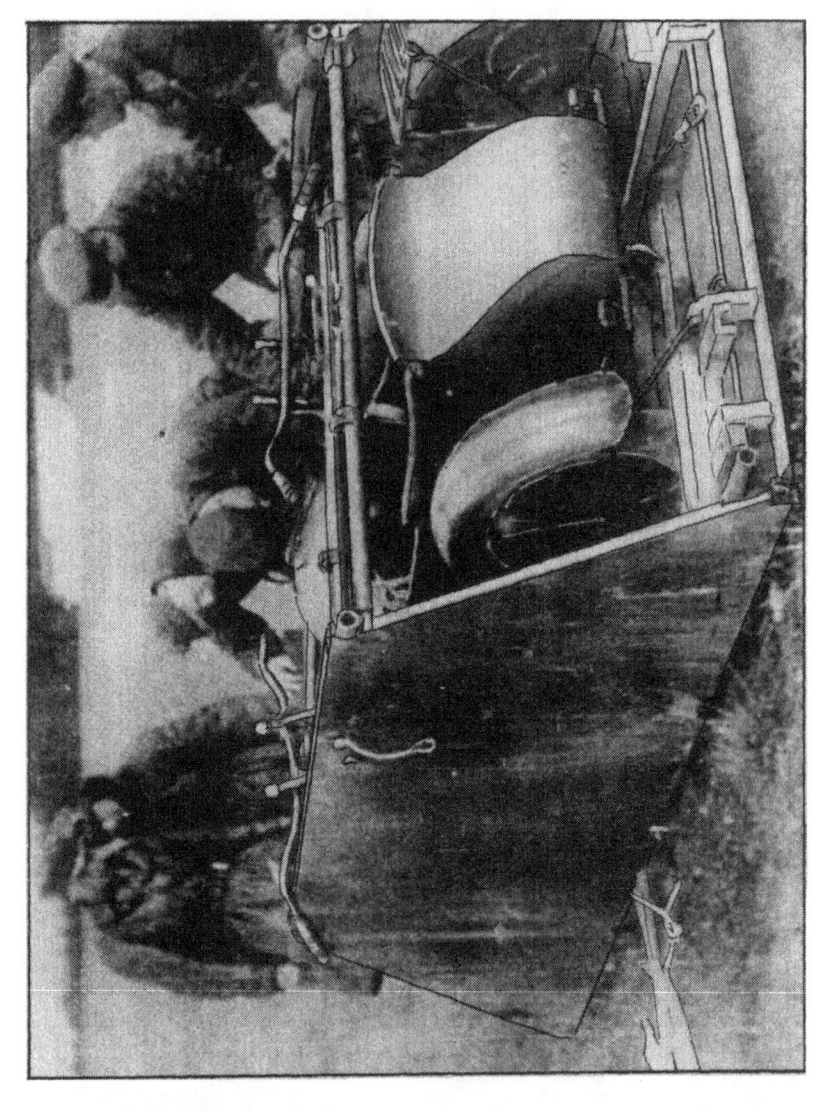

Fig. 3 Russian Crating gear for two M/c sidecars (Prc. 1939)

VI HEAVY DROPPING TECHNIQUES (ii)

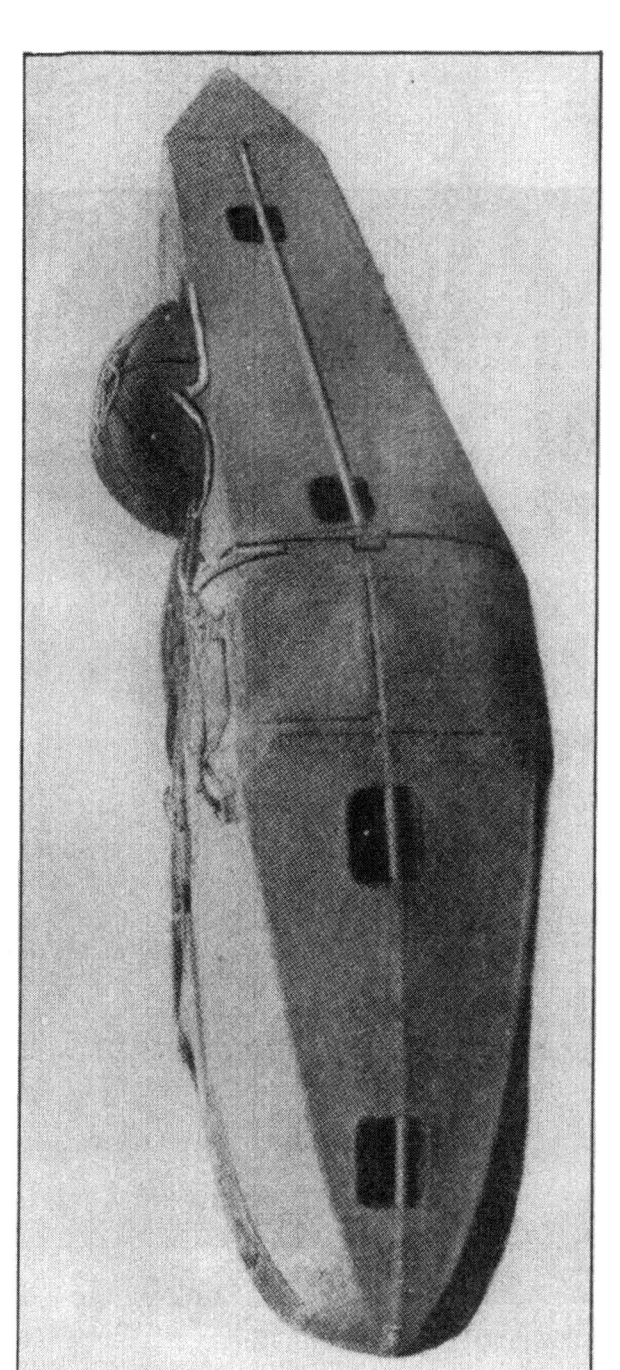

The steel frame with fabric cover hinges in the centre. The piece and the wheels are housed in the biggest end of the crate. The parachute strap is attached at four points.

Fig. 4 German Crating gear for 3.7 cm A. Tk. Gun

VI HEAVY DROPPING TECHNIQUES (ii)

Steel Frame hinges in half and is quickly detachable from the equipment. Note the standard heavy dropping attachments on the underside of J.U.-52

Fig. 5 German 10.5 cm. Recoilless Gun prepared for dropping

VI HEAVY DROPPING TECHNIQUES (iii)

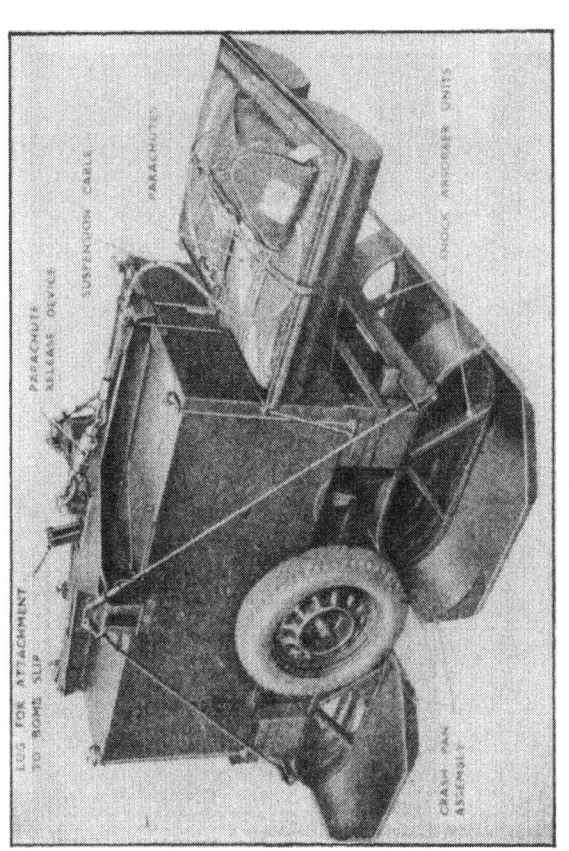

Dropped from bomb hook under Aircraft fuselage

Fig. 6   British Lt. Wt. trailer crated for dropping

VI HEAVY DROPPING TECHNIQUES (vii)

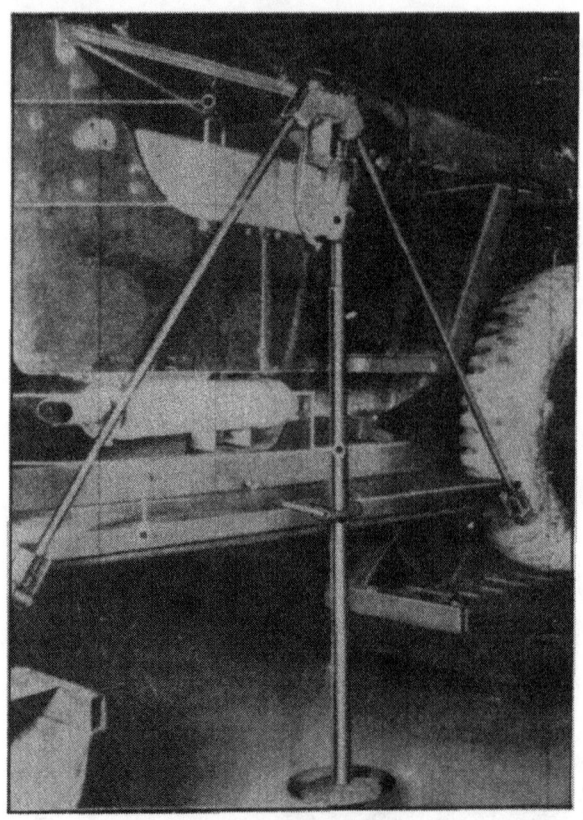

The release mechanism makes contact with the ground just before the Crash Pans and the compression of the rod opens the main hook attaching the parachute assembly to the equipment. This is to prevent equipment being dragged and damaged after landing.

Fig. 7   British Parachute Ground Release device (Heavy dropping)

VI HEAVY DROPPING TECHNIQUES (iii)

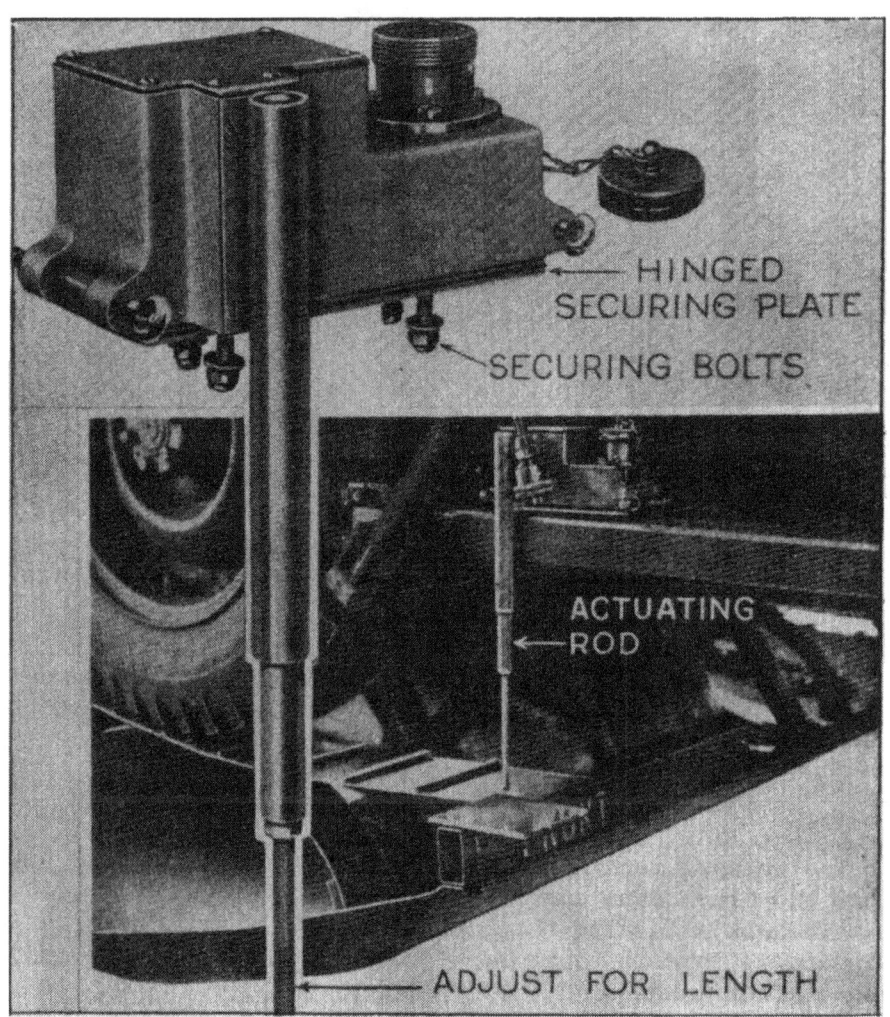

Fig. 8 Parachute ground release device (Heavy dropping)

VI HEAVY DROPPING TECHNIQUES (iv)

Heavy equipment may be attached direct to the bomb racks for heavy dropping. A more recent development is the use of an intermediary Heavy dropping beam.

Fig. 9   Jeep and Gun in Bomb bay of Halifax

VI HEAVY DROPPING TECHNIQUES (iv)

The Beam standardises and simplifies the suspension gear for heavy dropping.

Fig. 10 Heavy dropping Beam for Hastings

VI HEAVY DROPPING TECHNIQUES (iv)

3.7 cm. A. Tk. Gun loaded for dropping without crating gear.

Fig. 11   German Heavy dropping suspension Gear for JU-52

VI/12

VI HEAVY DROPPING TECHNIQUES (iv)

This equipment was also dropped in a steel frame crate. Note standard attachments for heavy dropping under JU-52 fuselage.

Fig. 12. German 2 cm. A.A. Gun prepared for dropping

VI HEAVY DROPPING TECHNIQUES (iv)

Note:— (a) Heavy dropping attachments under JU-52
(b) Stowage of the parachute in sidecar

Fig. 13 German Motor cycle-sidecar prepared for dropping

RESTRICTED

VI HEAVY DROPPING TECHNIQUES (v)

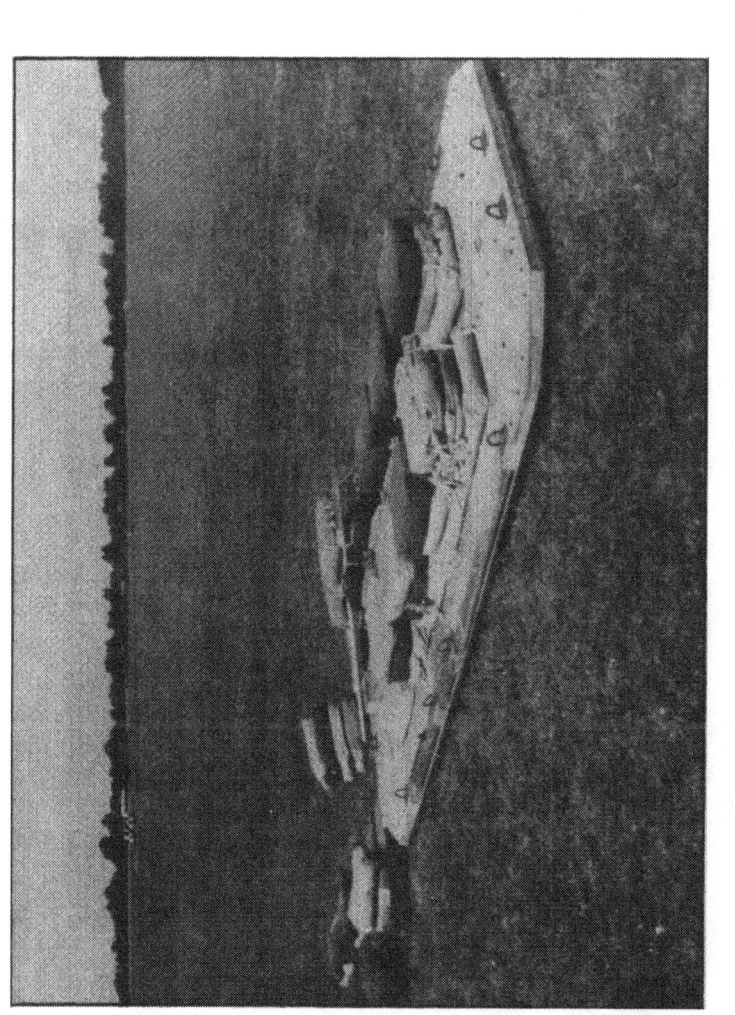

The weight of the board = 550 lbs. (approx.)
Packing (Wood shavings) arranged for dropping a Bren Gun Carrier

Fig. 14   British Pallet for Heavy dropping

RESTRICTED

VI HEAVY DROPPING TECHNIQUES (v)

Packing placed under all heavy members of chassis and suspension.

Fig. 15   15 cwt. Truck loaded on pallet

VI HEAVY DROPPING TECHNIQUES (v)

The wooden Trays contain the bagged parachutes before dropping.

Fig. 16   U.S.A. A.A. Gun on Pallet (Skid Board)

RESTRICTED

VI   HEAVY DROPPING TECHNIQUES (vi)

The packing used in this photograph of a Scout car on a pallet is vertical plywood. This type of packing is favoured in the U.S.A.

Fig. 17   U.S.A. Roller Conveyor for Aircraft

RESTRICTED

VI HEAVY DROPPING TECHNIQUES (vi)

Roller conveyor fitted in HASTINGS Aircraft. Two banks of stores may be air dispatched at the same time.

Fig. 18   British Roller Conveyor for HASTINGS

VI HEAVY DROPPING TECHNIQUES (vii)

Fig. 19   Pallet discharge by Gravity

VI HEAVY DROPPING TECHNIQUES (vii)

The loaded pallet is discharged from the aircraft by a ejector parachute. The main parachute is developed by means of a direct static line.

Fig. 20   U.S.A. Pallet discharge by EJECTOR parachute

RESTRICTED

VI HEAVY DROPPING TECHNIQUES (viii)

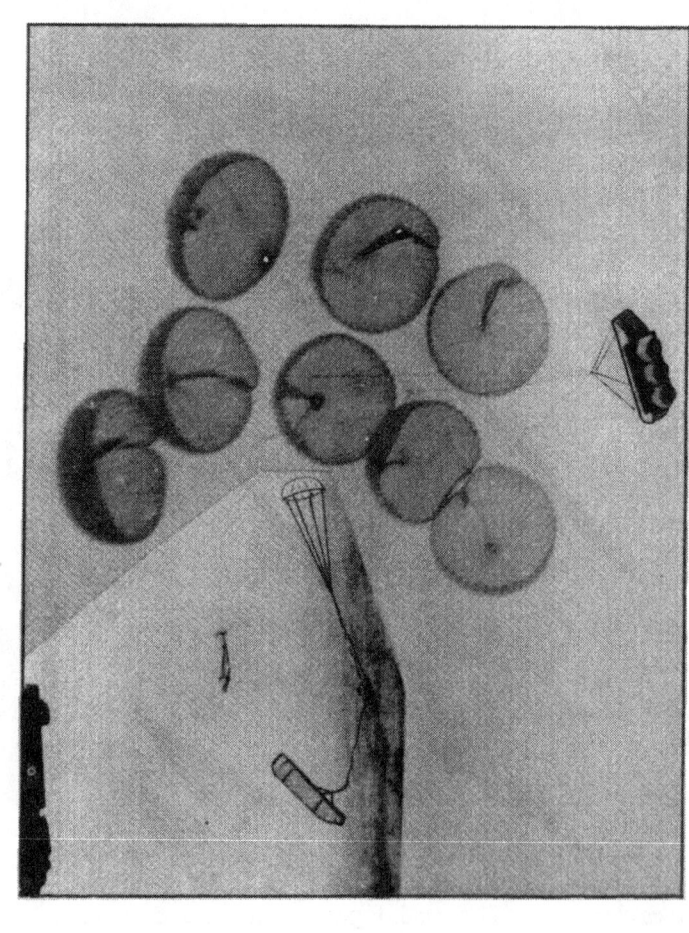

The doors on the underside of paratechnicon open, by means of a delay mechanism, eleven seconds after the box is released from the Aircraft. The opening of doors enables the percussion air bags to inflate.

Fig. 21   British Paratechnicon with eight 60 ft. parachutes

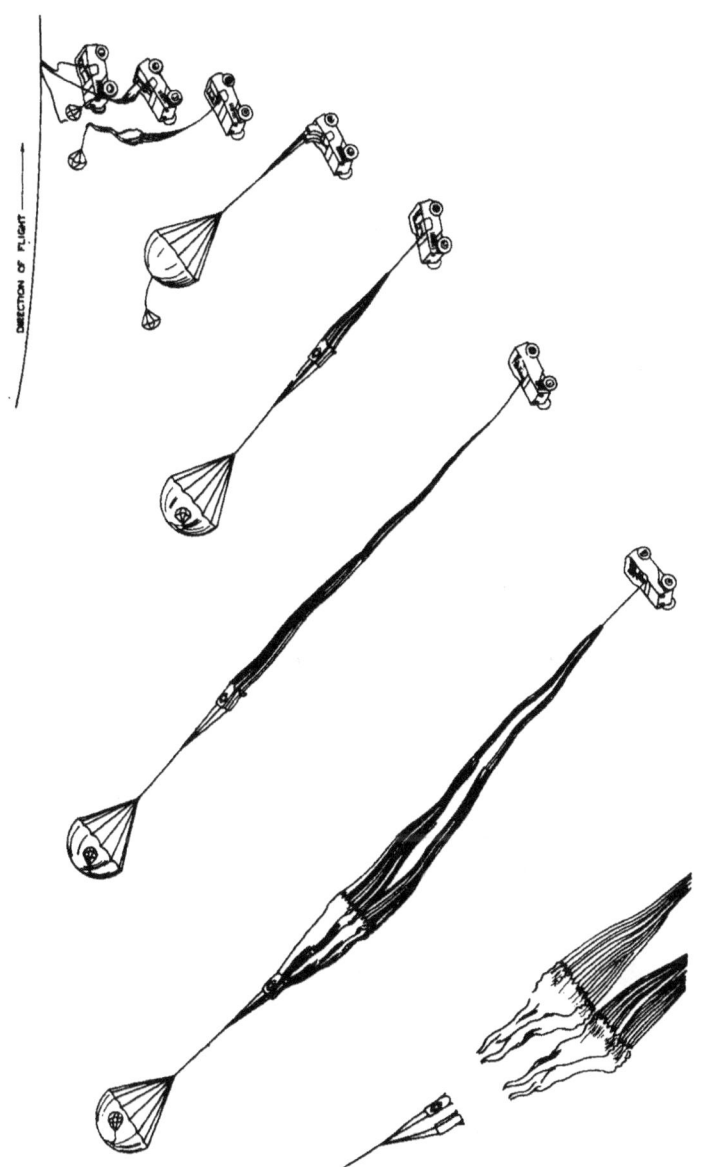

An AUXILIARY parachute developes a RETARDER parachute which in turn draws the bags from the MAIN canopies.

Fig. 22 A standard British Method of Heavy dropping

VI HEAVY DROPPING TECHNIQUES (ix)

An AUXILIARY parachute developes a RETARDER parachute which in turn draws the bags from the MAIN canopies.

Fig. 22   A standard British Method of Heavy dropping

VI HEAVY DROPPING TECHNIQUES (ix)

Fig. 23   Russian Heavy dropping (Pre. 1939)

VI HEAVY DROPPING TECHNIQUES (x)

The parachute is attached to the container for 2 M/C Sidecars (Pre. 1939 picture)

Fig. 24   Russian 130 ft. diameter heavy dropping parachute

VI HEAVY DROPPING TECHNIQUES (x)

Each parachute has only one auxiliary strop from the cluster centre point.

Fig. 25 Cluster of Twelve 32 ft. Flat Parachutes

VI HEAVY DROPPING TECHNIQUES (x)

Equipment is the British 6 pdr. gun. The rigging lines of each parachute are divided into four groups each with an auxiliary strop to the cluster centre point.

Fig. 26   Cluster of four 60 ft. flat parachutes

VI HEAVY DROPPING TECHNIQUES (x)

Eight 60 ft. parachutes attached by single strops to cluster centre.

Fig. 27   Example of parachutes splitting

VI HEAVY DROPPING TECHNIQUES (x)

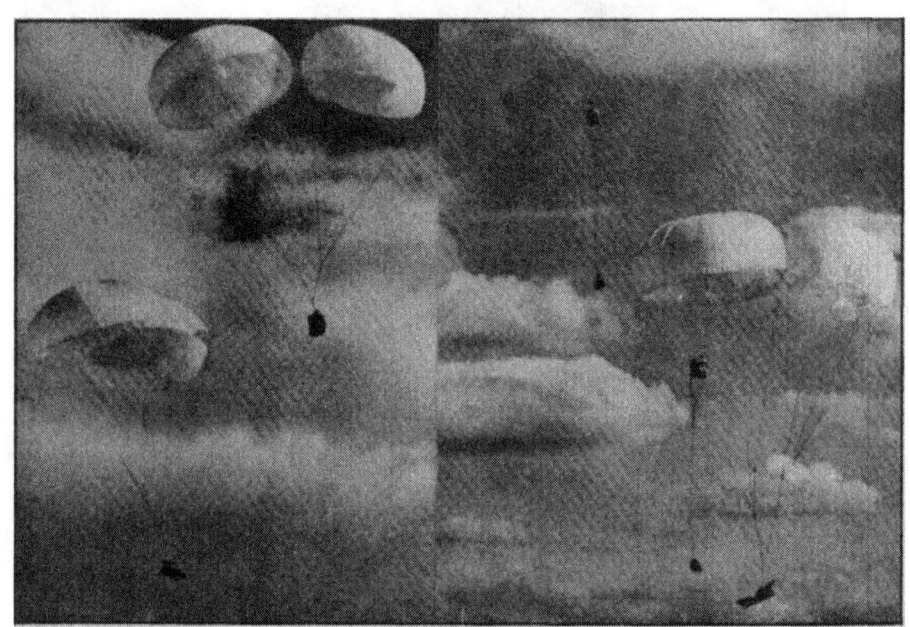

A Medium Howitzer (right) may be dropped by means of two 100 ft. parachutes. The undeveloped - (squidding) parachute is the discarded Ejector parachute.

Fig. 28   U.S.A. 100 ft. parachutes

SECTION VII

FREIGHTING

SECTION VII   AIRFREIGHTING ACCESSORIES

(i)   Aircraft load lashing examples and equipment.

(ii) Obsolete Russian suspension methods of airfreighting.

(iii) Aircraft loading ramps.

SECTION VII   AIRFREIGHTING ACCESSORIES

INDEX

(i)   Fig 1   A.A. Gun lashed in a DAKOTA
       Fig 2   25 pdr Fd Gun lashed in a C-119
       Fig 3   Lashings for Aircraft loads

(ii)   Fig 4   Russian T-27 'Tanket' suspended below TB-3

(iii) Fig 5   HASTINGS Light duty Ramp
       Fig 6   HASTINGS Heavy duty Ramp
       Fig 7   Nose Ramps of C-124 (Globemaster)

VII AIRFREIGHTING ACCESSORIES (i)

Note: (a) The spreaders for distributing the wheel loads over the fuselage floor.

(b) The Aircraft strong points to which the chain lashings are attached and the bottle screws for tightening.

Fig. 1   A.A. Gun lashed down in a 'Dakota'

RESTRICTED

VII AIRFREIGHTING ACCESSORIES (i)

Fig. 2   25 pdr. Fd. Gun lashed down in a C-119

RESTRICTED

VII AIRFREIGHTING ACCESSORIES (i)

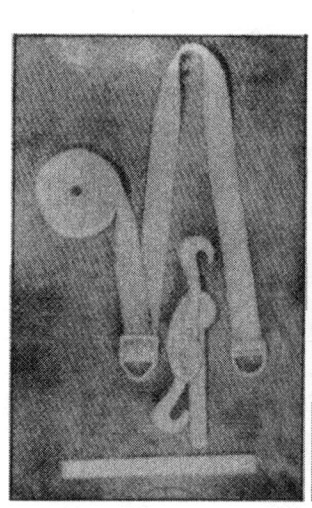

American
5000 lb
web lashing.

American 10,000 lb
chain lashing C.W.
C-2 tie down device :-
(A) Hook.
(B) Steel alloy chain.
(C) Chain attachment point.
(D) Tensioner.
(E) Quick release.

Fig. 3   Lashings for Aircraft Loads

VII/3

VII AIRFREIGHTING ACCESSORIES (ii)

Pre. 1939 - Tank and Aircraft now obsolete
Vehicles and guns were also freighted in a similar manner.
Fig. 4   Russian T.27 Tankct suspended below TB-3

RESTRICTED
VII AIRFREIGHTING ACCESSORIES (iii)   VII/5

Each ramp may be lifted by one man and they are included in the aircraft loading.

Fig. 5   "Hastings" light duty ramp

VII AIRFREIGHTING ACCESSORIES (iii)

The ramp may be jacked up on wheels for ease of movement about airfield. The ramp weighs over 3,000 lbs. and is not included in the aircraft loading.

The Aircraft is equipped with hand winches for the loading of equipment.

Fig. 6   "Hastings" heavy duty ramp

VII/7

VII AIRFREIGHTING ACCESSORIES (iii)

The ramps form part of the doors. The ease and speed of loading and unloading is very considerable compared to the Hastings. The Aircraft is equipped with power winches.

Fig. 7   Nose ramps of C-124 (Globemaster)

RESTRICTED

www.ingramcontent.com/pod-product-compliance
Lightning Source LLC
Chambersburg PA
CBHW060529090426

42735CB00011B/2431